Translation Theories Explored
Continuing *Translation Theories Explained*

Translation Theories Explored is a series designed to engage with the range and diversity of contemporary translation studies. Translation itself is as vital and as charged as ever . If anything, it has become more plural, more varied and more complex in today's world. The study of translation has responded to these challenges with vigour In recent decades the field has gained in depth, its scope continues to expand and it is increasingly interacting with other disciplines. The series sets out to reflect and foster these developments. It aims to keep track of theoretical developments, to explore new areas, approaches and issues, and generally to extend and enrich the intellectual horizon of translation studies. Special attention is paid to innovative ideas that may not as yet be widely known but deserve wider currency.

Individual volumes explain and assess particular approaches. Each volume combines an overview of the relevant approach with case studies and critical reflection, placing its subject in a broad intellectual and historical context, illustrating the key ideas with examples, summarizing the main debates, accounting for specific methodologies, achievements and blind spots, and opening up new perspectives for the future. Authors are selected not only on their close familiarity and personal af finity with a particular approach but also on their capacity for lucid exposition, critical assessment and imaginative thought.

The series is aimed at researchers and graduate students who wish to learn about new approaches to translation in a comprehensive but accessible way.

Theo Hermans
Series Editor

Translating as a Purposeful Activity

Functionalist Approaches Explained

Christiane Nord

ST JEROME

PUBLISHING

Manchester, UK & Kinderhook (NY), USA

First published in 1997
by St. Jerome Publishing
2 Maple Road West, Brooklands, Manchester M23 9HH, UK
Fax: +44 161 905 3498.
Email: stjerome@compuserve.com
www.stjerome.co.uk

Reprinted 2001, 2007, 2012

© 1997 Christiane Nord

ISBN 978-1900650-02-1 (pbk)
ISSN 1365-0513 (*Translation Theories Explored*)

Typeset by Delta Typesetters, Cairo, Egypt
Email: hilali1945@yahoo.co.uk

British Library Cataloguing in Publication Data
A catalogue record for this book is available from the British Library

Library of Congress Cataloging-in-Publication Data
Library of Congress Catalog Control Number 98-210143

Printed and bound in Great Britain by
4edge Limited, Hockley. www.4edge.co.uk

Contents

Introduction

Translating as a purposeful activity... isn't that stating the obvious? Aren't all human activities aimed at some purpose or other? What does it mean to say that translating (which here will always include interpreting unless stated otherwise) is a purposeful activity?

The title is not meant to tell you something you didn't know before; it's simply stating the aspects of translating that will be focused on in this book. The main title is evaluative rather than referential in function (these terms will be explained in chapter 4); the referential part is the subtitle 'Functionalist Approaches Explained'. This book thus explains functionalist approaches to translation. 'Functionalist' means focusing on the function or functions of texts and translations. Functionalism is a broad term for various theories that approach translation in this way, although what we will call *Skopostheorie* has played a major role in the development of this trend; a number of scholars subscribe to functionalism and draw inspiration from *Skopostheorie* without calling themselves anything like 'skopists'. We shall thus be looking at functionalism as a broad approach, trying to distinguish between its parts wherever possible and necessary.

Our title emphasizes that translating is an activity. This means that a theory of translation can be embedded in a theory of human action or activity. The parameters of action theory may help to explain some aspects of translation.

Human actions or activities are carried out by 'agents', individuals playing roles. When playing the role of senders in communication, people have communicative purposes that they try to put into practice by means of texts. Communicative purposes are aimed at other people who are playing the role of receivers. Communication takes place through a medium and in situations that are limited in time and place. Each specific situation determines what and how people communicate, and it is changed by people communicating. Situations are not universal but are embedded in a cultural habitat, which in turn conditions the situation. Language is thus to be regarded as part of culture. And communication is conditioned by the constraints of the situation-in-culture.

Example: If you ask a policeman for a particular street in Jakarta, he will give you an elaborate and very detailed description, even though he doesn't have the faintest idea where that particular street is. He just cannot say Sorry, I don't know , because that would mean losing face.

In translation, senders and receivers belong to different cultural groups in that they speak different languages. Non-verbal forms of behaviour may be different as well. Senders and receivers thus need help from someone who is familiar with both languages (and cultures) and who is willing to play the role of translator or intermediary between them. In professional settings, translators don't normally act on their own account; they are asked to intervene by either the sender or the receiver, or perhaps by a third person. From an observer's point of view, this third party will be playing the role of 'commissioner' or 'initiator'; from the translator's point of view, they will be the 'client' or 'customer'. Initiators may have communicative purposes of their own or they may share those of either the sender or the receiver. Translating thus involves aiming at a particular communicative purpose that may or may not be identical with the one that other participants have in mind.

Example: Suppose you are in Jakarta and you want to know how to find a particular street. You don't speak Indonesian; the policeman doesn't speak your language. So you ask your Indonesian friend to speak for you. Your friend turns to the policeman and after listening to his elaborate explanations where to turn right behind the next bus-stop, left at the level crossing, and then right again opposite the filling-station, she tells you, He doesn't know the way, we should ask someone else. (Your friend is familiar with the culture-specific non-verbal or verbal markers giving away the policeman's ignorance.) Or she tells you, 'You have to turn right behind the next bus-stop, left at the level crossing, and then right again opposite the filling-station, and there you will be in the street you are looking for'. (She interprets the policeman's behaviour as that of somebody who really knows the way.) In both cases your friend has clearly interpreted the policeman's utterance in situation-in-culture; she has translated the *function*, not the wording.

Although functionalist approaches draw on practical experience of the translation profession, they are not just descriptive; they do not merely describe what can be observed in the process of translation or the results of this process. As we will see later on, functionalism makes use of descriptive methods (for example, parallel text analysis) to locate and compare the communicative norms and conventions valid in various culture communities. Since functionalist approaches have been developed mainly within university translator-training institutions, they are normative or evaluative to the extent that they include the evaluation of translations with regard to their functionality in a given situation-in-culture; future professional translators must be trained not only to produce 'good' (that is, functional) translations

2

satisfying their customers' needs, but also to find good arguments to defend their products against unjustified criticism from clients and users. For example, your Indonesian friend might be reproached for not having told you exactly what the policeman said, since you have seen the policeman pointing in some direction and using many more words than would have been necessary just to say 'I don't know!'. What concepts should your Indonesian translator use to defend her decision?

This short introduction into the functionalist view of translation has already touched on the main aspects to be presented in the book. After a brief historical overview of how *Skopostheorie* and the general function-oriented concepts came into being (chapter 1) we will look at the main ideas of functionalist approaches. The agents and conditions of translational action will be explained and defined (chapter 2). The next step will be an analysis of the basic concepts of *Skopostheorie*, such as '*Skopos*'/'purpose', 'function', 'culture', 'equivalence/ adequacy' and 'text-type' (chapter 3). Then we will look at how the approach is applied in the training of professional translators, dealing with text functions, a functional typology of translations, norms and conventions in functional translation, a categorization of translation problems, functional translation units and some aspects of evaluation (chapter 4). Since some critics claim this model is not suited to the translation of literary texts, a further chapter will look more closely at functionalism in literary translation (chapter 5). The last chapter in this 'main ideas' part of the book will deal with functionalism in simultaneous interpreting (chapter 6).

Although some critical reactions to functionalism will be mentioned as we look at the main ideas, the main criticisms will be bundled together and discussed systematically in chapter 7. Being involved in functional translation teaching myself, my own attitude toward this approach will probably show through, despite all attempts at objectivity. So as not to hide anything, my personal version of functionalism will be presented quite briefly (chapter 8) before dealing with the current trends and future perspectives in functionalist theory (chapter 9).

The book concludes with a list of references including a commented bibliography of the main functionalist texts.

1. Historical Overview

The following pages describe the development of modern functionalism in translation studies. Of course, since functionalism didn't suddenly appear overnight, a brief description of early functionalist views of translation is needed in order to sketch the situation from which the more recent theories and methodologies emerged. We will then outline the landmarks of what is now often referred to as the 'German School' of functionalist translation theory: Katharina Reiss and functionalist translation criticism, Hans J. Vermeer's *Skopostheorie* and its extensions, Justa Holz-Mänttäri's theory of translational action, and a number of works oriented toward the use of functionalist methodology in translator training. The basic concepts of translational action and *Skopostheorie* will be analyzed in detail later on; this chapter is merely designed to give a chronological overview of authors and works.

Early Views

Functional approaches to translation were not invented in the twentieth century. Throughout history we find translators – mainly literary or Bible translators – observing that different situations call for different renderings. However, 'translation proper' is frequently associated with word-for-word fidelity to the source text, even though the result may not be considered appropriate for the intended purpose. Cicero (106-43 B.C.) described the dilemma as follows:

> If I render word for word, the result will sound uncouth, and if compelled by necessity I alter anything in the order or wording, I shall seem to have departed from the function of a translator. (*De optimo genere oratorum* v.14)

Many Bible translators have felt that the process of translating should involve both procedures: a faithful reproduction of formal source-text qualities in one situation and an adjustment to the target audience in another. Jerome (348-420) and Martin Luther (1483-1546) held the view that there are passages in the Bible where the translator must reproduce "even the word-order" (St. Jerome, *Letter to Pammachius*) or keep "to the letter" (Luther, *Circular Letter on Translation*, 1530); in other passages they believed it was more important "to render the sense" (St. Jerome) or to adjust the text to the target audience's needs and expectations.

In a similar vein, Eugene A. Nida (1964) distinguishes between formal

4

and dynamic equivalence in translation, 'formal equivalence' referring to a faithful reproduction of source-text form elements and 'dynamic equivalence' denoting equivalence of extralinguistic communicative effect:

> A translation of dynamic equivalence aims at complete naturalness of expression, and tries to relate the receptor to modes of behavior relevant within the context of his own culture; it does not insist that he understand the cultural patterns of the source-language context in order to comprehend the message. (Nida 1964:159)

In 'A Framework for the Analysis and Evaluation of Theories of Translation' (1976), Nida places special emphasis on the purpose of the translation, on the roles of both the translator and the receivers, and on the cultural implications of the translation process:

> When the question of the superiority of one translation over another is raised, the answer should be looked for in the answer to another question, 'Best for whom?'. The relative adequacy of different translations of the same text can only be determined in terms of the extent to which each translation successfully fulfills the purpose for which it was intended. In other words, the relative validity of each translation is seen in the degree to which the receptors are able to respond to its message (in terms of both form and content) in comparison with (1) what the original author evidently intended would be the response of the original audience and (2) how that audience did, in fact, respond. The responses can, of course, never be identical, for interlingual communication always implies some differences in cultural setting, with accompanying diversities in value systems, conceptual presuppositions, and historical antecedents. (1976:64f)

Nida calls his approach 'sociolinguistic'. However, when trying to apply it to translation in general, he suggests a three-stage model of the translation process. In this model, source-text surface elements (grammar, meaning, connotations) are analyzed as linguistic kernel or near-kernel structures that can be transferred to the target language and restructured to form target-language surface elements (cf. Nida 1976:75, also Nida and Taber 1969: 202f). This basically linguistic approach, whose similarity with Noam Chomsky's theory of syntax and generative grammar (1957, 1965) is not accidental, had more influence on the development of translation theory in Europe during the 1960s and 1970s than did the idea of dynamic equivalence.

A general focus on straight linguistics rather than dynamic functionalism is reflected in the importance Nida's work has been given in recent

5

surveys of modern translation theories (as in Larose 1989 and Gentzler 1993). For Gentzler (1993:46), Nida's work became "the basis upon which a new field of investigation in the twentieth century – the 'science of translation' – was founded". Given this emphasis, it is not surprising to find Gentzler allocating just two small paragraphs to what he calls 'the Reiss/ Vermeer approach', which he sums up in the following way:

> Reiss's work culminates in the co-authored *Grundlegung einer allgemeinen Translationstheorie*, written together with Hans J. Vermeer in 1984, in which they argue that translation should be governed primarily by the one functional aspect which predominates, or, in the new terminology, by the original's 'Skopos'... (1993:71).

One of the aims of the present book is to correct the impression caused by publications like Gentzler's, both with regard to authorship details and with respect to the relations between text typology (Reiss) and *Skopostheorie* (Vermeer). But we will come to this in due course.

The fact that the reception of Nida's approach focused on its linguistic implications must be understood in historical terms. Linguistics was perhaps the dominant humanistic discipline of the 1950s and 1960s. Early experiments with machine translation had to draw on contrastive representations of languages. The optimistic view that machine translation was feasible is reflected in Oettinger's definition of translation:

> Translating may be defined as the process of transforming signs or representations into other signs or representations. If the originals have some significance, we generally require that their images also have the same significance, or, more realistically, as nearly the same significance as we can get. Keeping significance invariant is the central problem in translating between natural languages. (1960:104)

At the same time, structuralist linguistics, along with the idea of language as a code and the conception of language universals, nourished the illusion that language – and translation as a linguistic operation – could be an object of strictly scientific investigation, on a par with any object in the natural sciences. Translation had previously been regarded as an art or a craft; now translation scholars were happy to have their activity recognized as a science and admitted to the inner circle of scholarly pursuits as a branch of applied linguistics. Many definitions of translation emphasized the linguistic aspect:

> Translation may be defined as follows: the replacement of textual

material in one language (SL) by equivalent material in another language (TL). (Catford 1965:20)

Translating consists in reproducing in the receptor language the closest natural equivalent of the source-language message. (Nida and Taber 1969:12)

These linguistic approaches basically saw translating as a code-switching operation. With the more pragmatic reorientation at the beginning of the 1970s, the focus shifted from the word or phrase to the text as a unit of translation, but the fundamental linguistic trend was not broken. Equivalence as a basic concept or even constituent of translation was never really questioned. For Wilss, for example,

Translation leads from a source-language text to a target-language text which is as close an equivalent as possible and presupposes an understanding of the content and style of the original. (Wilss 1977:70)

Equivalence-based linguistic approaches focused on the source text, the features of which had to be preserved in the target text. For Werner Koller,

there exists equivalence between a given source text and a given target text if the target text fulfils certain requirements with respect to these frame conditions. The relevant conditions are those having to do with such aspects as content, style and function. The *requirement* of equivalence thus has the following form: *quality (or qualities) X in the SL text must be preserved*. This means that the source-language content, form, style, function, etc. must be preserved, or at least that the translation must seek to preserve them as far as possible. (1979: 187; translation 1989:100, emphasis in the original)

This is a normative statement. It declares any target text that is not equivalent ("as far as possible") to the corresponding source text to be a nontranslation. Many theorists still adhere to this view, although some have had to recognize that there may be cases of non-equivalence in translation caused by the pragmatic differences between source and target cultures. We can see this in some of Koller's more recent work:

Ad-hoc cases of adaptation have to be regarded as text-producing elements in the translation process; they may be appropriate, or even inevitable, in order to make the translation reach its audience, i.e. from the point of view of pragmatic equivalence. (1992:235, my translation)

For Koller, such adaptations do not mean that the requirement of equivalence between the source and target texts has been abandoned. What has happened to it then? The borderline between 'translation with elements of text revision' (= equivalence) and 'text revision with translated elements' (= non-equivalence) (Koller 1995:206ff) seems to have become a question of quantities. The equivalence approach lacks consistency: some scholars praise literalism as the optimum procedure in translation (Newmark 1984/85:16); others, such as Koller, allow a certain number of adaptive procedures, para-phrases or other non-literal procedures in specific cases where, as Koller puts it, "they are intended to convey implicit source-text values or to improve the comprehensibility of the text for the target audience" (1993:53; my translation). These rather arbitrary criteria do not account for the fact that implicit values should remain implicit in some cases, nor do they recognize that comprehensibility is not a general purpose common to all texts or text-types.

The theorists of equivalence tend to accept non-literal translation proce-dures more readily in the translation of pragmatic texts (instructions for use, advertisements) than in literary translation. Different or even contra-dictory standards for the selection of transfer procedures are thus set up for different genres or text-types. This makes the equivalence approach rather confusing.

Summing up the theorizing of translation over the centuries, Kelly states:

> A translator moulds his image of translation by the function he as-signs to language; from function, one extrapolates to nature. Thus those who translate merely for objective information have defined translation differently from those for whom the source text has a life of its own. (1979:4)

This may be the reason why some translation scholars working in training institutions started to give functionalist approaches priority over equivalence-based approaches. Quite simply, they started to look at the profession for which they were training. They found that professional translating includes many cases where equivalence is not called for at all. In the translation of a British school certificate for a German university, for example, the target text is not expected to look like, or function as, a German school certificate.

In this situation, some scholars became increasingly dissatisfied with the relationship between translation theory and practice. A new theory was called for.

Katharina Reiss and the Functional Category of Translation Criticism

As early as 1971 Katharina Reiss (written Reiß in German) introduced a functional category into her 'objective approach to translation criticism'. Although still firmly within equivalence-based theory, her book *Möglichkeiten und Grenzen der Übersetzungskritik* (Possibilities and Limits of Translation Criticism) may be regarded as the starting point for the scholarly analysis of translation in Germany. Taking equivalence as her basis, Reiss develops a model of translation criticism based on the functional relationship between source and target texts. According to Reiss, the ideal translation would be one "in which the aim in the TL [target language] is equivalence as regards the conceptual content, linguistic form and communicative function of a SL [source-language] text" (1977, translation in 1989:112). She refers to this kind of translation as "integral communicative performance" ([1977] 1989:114).

In 1971 Katharina Reiss was already an experienced translator herself, having translated works from Spanish into German, among them José Ortega y Gasset's famous essay *Miseria y esplendor de la traducción* (Misery and Splendour of Translation). She knew that real life presents situations where equivalence is not possible and, in some cases, not even desired. Her objective approach to translation criticism (cf. Nord 1996b) thus accounts for certain exceptions from the equivalence requirement. These exceptions are due to the specifications of what we will be referring to as the 'translation brief' (*Übersetzungsauftrag*). One exception is when the target text is intended to achieve a purpose or function other than that of the original. Examples include adapting a prose text for the stage, translating Shakespeare's plays for foreign-language classes, or providing word-for-word translations of an Arabic poem intended to serve as a basis for a free rendering by an English poet who does not know the source language. A further exception is when the target text addresses an audience different from the intended readership of the original. Examples include translating *Gulliver's Travels* for children and various forms of ideological editing motivated by religious, ethical or commercial criteria.

Reiss excludes these cases from the area of 'translation proper' and suggests they be referred to as 'transfers' (*Übertragungen*) (1971:105). In such situations the functional perspective takes precedence over the normal standards of equivalence. The translation critic can no longer rely on features derived from source-text analysis but has to judge whether the target text is functional in terms of the translation context. Thus, for Reiss,

It goes without saying that all the types of translation mentioned may be justified in particular circumstances. An interlinear version can be extremely useful in comparative linguistic research. Grammar translation is a good aid to foreign language learning. Learned translation is appropriate if one wishes to focus on the different means whereby given meanings are verbally expressed in different languages. And the changing of a text's function, as a verbal component within a total communicative process, may also be a justified solution. However, when the translation is an end in itself, in the sense of simply seeking to extend an originally monolingual communicative process to include receivers in another language, then it must be conceived as an integral communicative performance, which without any extratextual additions (notes, explanations etc.) provides an insight into the cognitive meaning, linguistic form and communicative function of the SL text. ([1977] 1989:114f)

In Reiss and Vermeer (1984), Katharina Reiss presents her idea of correlating text type and translation method as a 'specific theory' to be fitted into the framework of Vermeer's general theory of translation (see chapter 3 below). In this context, the status of her 'functional category' is changed. Since functional equivalence is no longer regarded as the normal aim of translation, the analysis of text types can no longer provide the decisive criteria for methodological choices. The classification of the source text as belonging to a particular text-type is thus relevant only in special cases where the intended function of the target text is to represent a textual equivalent of the source text. These cases are referred to as 'communicative' or 'imitating translations' in Reiss and Vermeer (1984:89f).

Hans J. Vermeer: *Skopostheorie* and Beyond

Hans J. Vermeer has gone much further in trying to bridge the gap between theory and practice. Having been trained as an interpreter (by Katharina Reiss!) he took up general linguistics (Vermeer 1972) then translation studies. His desire to break with linguistic translation theory developed from work published in 1976 and became very clear in his 'Framework for a General Translation Theory' of 1978. Vermeer states his general position as follows:

> Linguistics alone won't help us. First, because translating is not merely and not even primarily a linguistic process. Secondly, because linguistics has not yet formulated the right questions to tackle our problems. So let's look somewhere else. (1987a:29)

Vermeer ([1978] 1983b:49) considers translation (including interpreting) to be a type of transfer where communicative verbal and non-verbal signs are transferred from one language into another (other types would include the transfer from pictures to music, or from a blueprint to a building.) Translation is thus also a type of human action. In accordance with action theory (cf. von Wright 1968, Rehbein 1977, Harras 1978), Vermeer defines human action as intentional, purposeful behaviour that takes place in a given situation; it is part of the situation at the same time as it modifies the situation ([1978] 1983b:49). Further, since situations are embedded in cultures, any evaluation of a particular situation, of its verbalized and non-verbalized elements, depends on the status it has in a particular culture system. This is made clear in an illustration given by Vermeer himself:

> Suppose we were to observe an Indian getting up in the morning. We see him get out of bed, take a shower, brush his teeth and cleanse his mouth, put on clean clothes, pray, take a cup of tea and so on. If we asked him to describe his behaviour he would mention his shower (which he'd call a 'bath', if he speaks English) and perhaps forget about the tea. Suppose now, we would also observe a German during his morning ritual. We would see much the same procedure, although with certain differences in the way he would take his shower and put on his clothes; he, too, would have his breakfast (and perhaps brush his teeth afterwards). Asked about his behaviour he would certainly not forget to mention his 'buttered bread and coffee' and just as certainly would forget about his brushing his teeth. The descriptions of the two individuals from two different cultures would differ to a greater or lesser extent, but they would be culturally equivalent, both being considered natural behavioural acts with the same 'function' in their respective culture specific settings. (1987a:29)

For this line of thought, translation cannot be considered a one-to-one transfer between languages. Within the framework of such a comprehensive theory of human communication, a translation theory cannot draw on a linguistic theory alone, however complex it may be. What is needed is a theory of culture to explain the specificity of communicative situations and the relationship between verbalized and non-verbalized situational elements.

In Vermeer's approach, translation is a form of translational action based on a source text, which may consist of verbal and/or non-verbal elements (illustrations, plans, tables, etc.). Other forms of translational action may involve actions like a consultant giving information. This general frame is explained as follows:

> Any form of translational action, including therefore translation it-
> self, may be conceived as an action, as the name implies. Any action
> has an aim, a purpose. [...] The word *skopos*, then, is a technical term
> for the aim or purpose of a translation. [...] Further: an action leads to
> a result, a new situation or event, and possibly to a 'new' object.
> (Vermeer 1989b:173f)

This is why Vermeer calls his theory *Skopostheorie*, a theory of purposeful action. In the framework of this theory, one of the most important factors determining the purpose of a translation is the addressee, who is the in-tended receiver or audience of the target text with their culture-specific world-knowledge, their expectations and their communicative needs. Every translation is directed at an intended audience, since to translate means 'to produce a text in a target setting for a target purpose and target addressees in target circumstances" (Vermeer 1987a:29).

Note that the phrase we have just cited from Vermeer makes no mention of the source text. The status of the source is clearly much lower in *Skopostheorie* than in equivalence-based theories. While Reiss declares that the source text is the measure of all things in translation (Reiss 1988:70), Vermeer regards it as an 'offer of information' that is partly or wholly turned into an 'offer of information' for the target audience (cf. Vermeer 1982).

Skopostheorie was developed as the foundation for a *general* theory of translation able to embrace theories dealing with specific languages and cultures. In Reiss and Vermeer (1984), Katharina Reiss's concept of a rela-tionship between text type and translation method is integrated as a specific theory within the framework of Vermeer's general theory. It is important to note, however, that Part 1 (Vermeer's basic theory) and Part 2 (Reiss's spe-cific theories) do not really form a homogeneous whole.

We shall look at the main concepts of *Skopostheorie* in greater detail later on. In the meantime our task is to consider a few of the other major contributions to the development of functionalist theory.

Justa Holz-Mänttäri and the Theory of Translational Action

Justa Holz-Mänttäri, a Finland-based German professional translator, trans-lation scholar and teacher of prospective professional translators, goes one step further than Vermeer. In her theory and methodology of 'translational action' (*translatorisches Handeln*), first presented in 1981 and published in more elaborate form in 1984, she even avoids using the term 'translation' in the strict sense. This enables her to move away from the traditional concepts and expectations connected with the word. Her theory is based on the principles of action theory (von Wright 1968, Rehbein 1977) and is designed to cover all forms of intercultural transfer, including those which do not involve any source or target *texts*. She prefers to speak of 'message transmitters' (*Botschaftsträger*), which consist of textual material combined with other media such as pictures, sounds and body movements.

In Holz-Mänttäri's model, translation is defined as "a complex action designed to achieve a particular purpose" (Holz-Mänttäri and Vermeer 1985:4). The generic term for this phenomenon is 'translational action'. The purpose of translational action is to transfer messages across culture and language barriers by means of message transmitters produced by experts. Translators are experts in producing appropriate message transmitters in intercultural or transcultural communication or, as Holz-Mänttäri puts it, 'cooperation':

> Translational action is the process of producing a message transmitter
> of a certain kind, designed to be employed in superordinate action
> systems in order to coordinate actional and communicative coopera-
> tion. (1984:17, my translation)

Holz-Mänttäri places special emphasis on the actional aspects of the translation process, analyzing the roles of the participants (initiator, translator, user, message receiver) and the situational conditions (time, place, medium) in which their activities take place. One of her prime concerns is the status of translators in a world characterized by the division of labour. Her concepts of vocational training emphasize the role of translators as experts in their field. We will deal with these aspects in greater detail in the next chapter.

In more recent publications Justa Holz-Mänttäri draws on biocybernetics in order to explain the conditions which enable human individuals as social beings to get 'in tune with each other' for cooperation (1988:39). The ability to produce or *design* functional message transmitters is determined by brain functions, which have to be taken into account in the training of expert text designers (1993:304ff.). Since this approach can be seen as belonging to the area of cognitive and psycholinguistic translation studies, it will not be included in our study.

Functionalist Methodology in Translator Training

Right from the outset, *Skopostheorie* and the theory of translational action have had a considerable impact on the methodology of translator training. Hans G. Hönig and Paul Kussmaul (Kußmaul in German), both engaged in translator training at the Department of Applied Linguistics and Culture Science at Germersheim (University of Mainz, Germany), gave the starting signal with the publication of their book *Strategie der Übersetzung* (Translation Strategy) in 1982. Basing their method on action-oriented and culture-oriented communication theory, they show how functional strategies lead to appropriate solutions to translation problems. Although their examples are taken from German-English translating, the problems they discuss are clearly not language-specific but may occur, with slight variations due to language structures and culture conventions, in any translation situation. One of the basic principles defended by Hönig and Kussmaul is the "maxim of the necessary degree of precision" (1982:58ff.), which seems to be in line with Grice's well known conversational maxims of relevance and quantity (1975). It says "Try to reproduce just that semantic feature or just those features which is/are relevant in a given context with regard to the function of your translation" (Kussmaul 1995:92). Hönig and Kussmaul have both made numerous contributions to functionalist translator training.

In recent publications Hönig and Kussmaul draw heavily on empirical psycholinguistic methods for analyzing mental and cognitive processes (Think-Aloud Protocols) in order to gain a better understanding of creativity (Kussmaul 1993, 1995) and of the translator's personality (Hönig 1993, 1995).

A feature common to the functionalist scholars engaged in translator training is that, unlike the linguistic theorists, they try to focus on the language-independent pragmatic or cultural aspects of translation, emphasizing the specific nature of translation competence as against language proficiency.

As a trained translator teaching translation at the Institute for Translating and Interpreting of Heidelberg University, I also had language-independent aspects of translation in mind when elaborating my 'translation-oriented model of text analysis in translation' (Nord [1988] 1991). My model includes the analysis of extratextual and intratextual aspects of the communicative action; it is designed to identify the function-relevant elements in both the existing source text and the prospective target text as defined by the translation brief. By comparing the *Skopos* with the source-text functions *before* starting to translate, translators should be able to locate the problems that will arise in the translating process. They should thus be able to devise a holistic strategy for their solution (cf. Nord 1996a).

Other translation scholars who draw on functionalism will be mentioned in the course of the following chapters.

2. Translating and the Theory of Action

Let's start by looking at a few examples:

A. The family is sitting at the breakfast table. Ben, the two-year-old baby, seems very excited and exclaims, pointing at his father, who is munching his toast: "Dada, mumumum, zzzzzz!" Then the father asks, "What's he saying?" Mother: "You've just eaten a fly!"

B. A young Portuguese girl wants to apply for a job in Germany and asks Mr T, a professional translator, to render her school reports into German for the prospective employer. Mr T translates the marks literally, rendering "14 valores" as "14 Werte", adding a note to explain that in the Portuguese marking system 20 is the best mark and 10 means 'failed'. (Example adapted from Vermeer 1989a:43)

C. In the closing plenary of a conference, the chairperson says in English: "Thank you, Mister Sloan, for your statement and for your invitation to Tennessee. Now, Mister Kao, will you please be so kind." The simultaneous interpreter in the German booth: "Vielen Dank, Herr Sloan, für diese Erklärung und für die Einladung nach Tennessee. Als nächstes zu Wort gemeldet ist: Herr Professor Kao." Note that the representative of a US entrepreneurs' association has remained "Herr Sloan" while Mister Kao, from the University of Toronto, is addressed as "Herr Professor Kao". (Example from Pöchhacker 1995:42f)

D. Ms Jones is a professional translator living in Spain. Her native language is English, but before coming to Spain she lived in Singapore for many years. One day, señor Fulano asks her for some advice. He has to write a business letter to a firm in Singapore but he doesn't know English. He has drafted the letter in Spanish. Could Mrs Jones translate it into English? Or would it be better to write in Chinese? Mrs Jones discusses the matter briefly with señor Fulano. She takes down the names and addresses of both señor Fulano and the Singapore firm, asks whether señor Fulano has brought the official writing paper. They agree on deadline, payment and so on. (Example adapted from Vermeer 1989a:38)

E. A German tourist in London asks a friendly-looking middle-aged lady: "Entschuldigen Sie bitte, können Sie mir sagen, wo die Nationalgalerie ist?" The lady shrugs her shoulders; she doesn't speak German. A passer-by, who happens to understand German, comes to her aid: "He's asking you for the way to the National Gallery; I'll tell him how to get there." Turning to the tourist he explains in German what bus to take and where to get off. The German says "Danke!" to the helpful mediator, "Sank you!" to the mute lady, and walks away in the direction indicated.

Each of these examples describes a situation where two or more people cannot communicate directly because of language barriers. Communication is established with the help of an intermediary. In all the examples except A the participants belong to different cultures or language communities and we can call the intermediary a 'translator' (here used as a generic term including interpreters). In cases B, C, and D, the intermediaries are professionals; in E, the intermediary is an untrained or 'natural' translator.

In the following sections we will take a closer look at these forms of communication across language and culture barriers, at the agents involved in intercultural communication, and at the situations in which intercultural communication takes place.

Translating as a Form of Translational Interaction

Communicative situations are settings in which people interact. Communication is thus interpersonal interaction and, as such, a variety of action. This is why action theory may be able to explain certain aspects of translation (cf. Holz-Mänttäri 1984, Vermeer 1986a, Nord 1988a, Ammann 1989c).

Action is the process of acting, which means "intentionally (at will) bringing about or preventing a change in the world (in nature)" (von Wright 1968:38). Action can thus be defined as an intentional "change or transition from one state of affairs to another" (cf. von Wright 1963:28). If generalized to cases where there are two or more agents, the theory of action can become a theory of *inter*action.

Human interaction may be described as an intentional change of a state of affairs affecting two or more people or agents. An interaction is referred to as 'communicative' when it is carried out through signs produced intentionally by one agent, usually referred to as the 'sender', and directed toward another agent, referred to as the 'addressee' or the 'receiver' (these terms will be distinguished below).

Communicative interactions take place in situations that are limited in time and space. This means every situation has historical and cultural dimensions that condition the agents' verbal and non-verbal behaviour, their knowledge and expectations of each other, their appraisal of the situation, and the standpoint from which they look at each other and at the world.

Within a particular culture community the situations of sender and receiver generally overlap enough for communication to take place (except for special occasions like the one described in example A above). When senders and receivers belong to different cultures, the situations can be so different that they need an intermediary who enables them to communicate across time and space.

Translators enable communication to take place between members of different culture communities. They bridge the gap between situations where differences in verbal and non-verbal behaviour, expectations, knowledge and perspectives are such that there is not enough common ground for the sender and receiver to communicate effectively by themselves. As we have seen in example E above, where the German tourist was helped by a passer-by, the translator's mediatory role does not always involve translating in any literal way. In fact, translators quite regularly do much more than translate texts: Ms Jones (in example D) might have advised señor Fulano to have the letter translated into Chinese by her colleague Mr Wang, who lives down the road. Thanks to her stay in Singapore she knows that people sometimes do not speak English very fluently in very small firms like the one señor Fulano wants to write to. When she gives this advice she is acting as a translator, even though she is not translating any text. To account for this difference we will distinguish between 'translational action' (the range of what translators actually do) and 'translation' (what they do when rendering texts).

Translating in the narrower sense always involves the use of some kind of source text, whereas translational action may involve giving advice and perhaps even *warning against* communicating in the intended way. Translational action may be carried out by a 'culture consultant' (Ammann 1990, Löwe 1989:105ff) or could include the tasks of a cross-cultural technical writer (Ammann and Vermeer 1990:27), as in the following situation:

Example: A translator receives operating instructions written in English that are full of mistakes and errors. He is asked to translate them into German. Instead of translating the faulty source text, the translator asks an engineer to tell him how the machine works and he then writes operating instructions in German. (cf. Nord [1988] 1991:27)

Bringing together these very rudimentary considerations, Figure 1 shows the relations between the concepts of action, interaction, translational action and translation. This network of concepts should explain the most important features of translation as interaction.

17

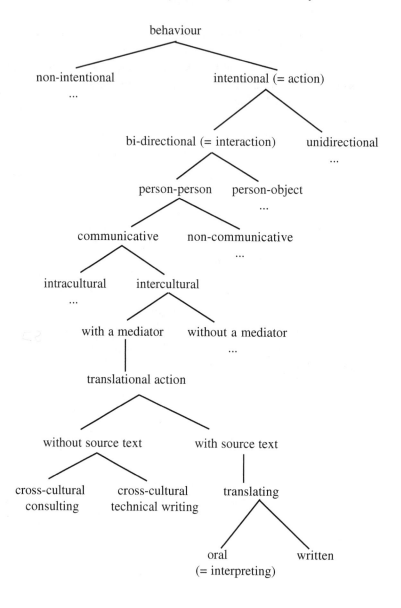

Figure 1. Translation as a Form of Mediated Intercultural Communication

We see that this approach essentially involves viewing translation as an intentional, interpersonal, partly verbal intercultural interaction based on a source text (cf. Vermeer 1989b:173). In the following sections we will look a little more closely at these defining features.

Translating as Intentional Interaction

When we speak of intentionality in an interaction, we assume there was a choice to act one way or another, to refrain from acting in a particular way, or to not act at all (cf. Vermeer 1986a:220). Vermeer defines the concept of action as follows:

> For an act of behaviour to be called an action the person performing it must (potentially) be able to explain *why* he acts as he does although he could have acted otherwise. (1989b:176)

Vermeer places particular emphasis on the fact that even *not acting* can be a form of action if it is in a situation where a visible action would have been possible. This is virtually the same as what Watzlawick says about behaviour:

> There is no negation of behaving. To put it even more simply, it is impossible *not* to behave one way or another. Whether you do something or refrain from doing it, whether you speak or keep silent, your behaviour will tell others something, influence them, communicate; others cannot help but react to your behaviour and will thus communicate in turn. (Watzlawick et al. 1972:51; my translation)

When we say translation is an intentional interaction we mean it is first and foremost *intended* to change an existing state of affairs (minimally, the inability of certain people to communicate with each other). There may be further intentions of a more strictly communicative nature, such as to inform the target addressees about something the source-text sender has to say.

Intentionality may be associated with the translator or, more often, with the person who is the 'initiator' of the translation process. Translational intention may or may not be similar to the intention guiding the original sender or text producer in the production of the source text.

Vermeer repeatedly emphasizes that 'intentionality' does not refer to an action really *being* intentional, but to its being seen or *interpreted as intentional* by the participants or any observer (1986a:220, 1990:51f). Of course, as Ammann points out (1989c:31), such interpretations may be quite different from what was actually meant by the person carrying out the action.

Translating as Interpersonal Interaction

The people or agents involved in the interaction have certain functions or roles. These roles are interconnected through a complex network of mutual relations. In order to understand this functional network we must analyze the roles in a little more detail. We shall start from a schematic representation of the translation process.

In the professional practice of intercultural communication, translators rarely start working of their own accord. They are usually called upon to do so by a client. In this context we may refer to the client as an 'initiator' who needs a particular text for a particular purpose and for a receiver in the target culture. The client asks the translator for a translation of a text and/or other information that the client regards as a suitable source. This source material has been produced by a text-producer and/or transmitted by a sender for a receiver under the conditions of the source culture. The process of translating (in the narrower sense) thus involves the main agents or roles of initiator and translator. The source-text producer only participates indirectly, being responsible for no more than the features of the source text. The receivers of both the source and the target texts, in their roles as addressees, are relevant for specification of the respective purposes of the two texts.

Further roles could be included in this model. Holz-Mänttäri (1984:109ff), for example, adds the *commissioner* and the final *user* of the target text. We will now look at all these roles in greater detail.

The Roles of Initiator and Commissioner

The initiator is the person, group or institution that starts off the translation process and determines its course by defining the purpose for which the target text is needed (cf. Nord [1988] 1991:8).

Example: A Portuguese student wants to study at a German university. German law requires school reports to be presented in German. The German legislative power is therefore the institutional initiator of the translation process. (Example adapted from Vermeer 1986a:274)

Holz-Mänttäri (1984:109f) distinguishes between the initiator (*Initiator* or *Bedarfsträger*), who actually needs the target text, and the commissioner (*Besteller, Auftraggeber*), who asks the translator to produce a target text for a particular purpose and addressee (similarly Vermeer 1986a:274). The commissioner may influence the very production of the target text, perhaps by demanding a particular text format or terminology.

The role of initiator may be taken on by any one of the agents in translational interaction. The source-text author, the prospective target-text receiver or the commissioner may all want to have the source text translated, for different reasons and for different purposes.

The Role of Translator

The role of the translator is crucial in the translation process. The translator is ostensibly the expert in translational action and should be responsible both for carrying out the commissioned task and for ensuring the result of the translation process, even when aspects like formatting and layout are assigned to other agents (cf. Vermeer 1989b:174). In the course of the translation process, the translator first acts as a receiver of both the translation brief (the commissioner's instructions) and the source text. After agreeing with the commissioner on the conditions involved, the translator produces a target text that they regard as functional in the sense that it meets the demands of the translation brief (cf. Vermeer 1989a:64). According to Vermeer, the translator's task is to

- analyze the acceptability and viability of the translation brief in legal, economic or ideological terms;
- check whether the translation is really needed;
- specify the activities required for carrying out the brief;
- perform a translational action, which may result in a target text, perhaps a short summary of the source text or, in special cases, in advising the client not to have the source text translated because a translation would not serve the intended purpose (cf. Vermeer 1986a:276, also Holz-Mänttäri 1984:109f).

The Role of Source-Text Producer

The source-text producer has produced the text that is to serve as the source for a translational action. The production of the source text may have been motivated by the need for a text in a particular translation process or by other factors that have nothing to do with translation. In the latter case, the source-text producer is not an immediate agent in the translational action.

Nord ([1988] 1991:42f), working in the field of written communication, makes a distinction between the sender and the text producer. The sender of the text is the person, group or institution that uses the a text in order to convey a certain message; the text producer is the one actually responsible for any linguistic or stylistic choices present in the text expressing the sender's communicative intentions. Although both roles are often carried out by the one person (as in literary works, textbooks or newspaper commentaries), the distinction may be relevant in cases where the sender's intention is not expressed adequately in the text. The translator can be compared with a target-culture text producer expressing a source-culture sender's communicative intentions.

The Role of Target-Text Receiver

The intended target-text receiver is the addressee of the translation and is thus a decisive factor in the production of the target text (Holz-Mänttäri 1984:111). The definition of the target-text receiver should be part of the translation brief, as will be explained shortly.

We may make a distinction between addressee and receiver. The addressee is the prospective receiver seen from the text producer's standpoint; the receiver is the person, group or institution that actually reads or listens to the text after it has been produced.

As is pointed out in Reiss and Vermeer (1984:101), information about the target-text addressee (with regard to sociocultural background, expectations, sensitivity or world knowledge) is of crucial importance for the translator, who should insist on receiving as many details as possible from the commissioner (similarly Nord [1988] 1991:9).

The Role of Target-Text User

Holz-Mänttäri (1984:111) describes the user of the target text (*Applikator*) as the one who finally puts it to use, perhaps as training material, as a source of information or as a means of advertising (similarly Vermeer 1986a:278).

It is important to note that different agent roles may be fulfilled by the one person, as is shown in the following examples:

Example: A translator has translated a novel written by a foreign author and asks a publisher to include it in the publication list. In this case the translator is the initiator, the commissioner and the translator in one person. (example from Vermeer 1986a:279)

Example: A German professor of medicine has to give a talk at an international conference where the official language will be English. The professor writes a German draft of the lecture; a translator translates it into English; the professor reads it at the conference. In this case, the professor is source-text producer, initiator and target-text user all in one person. (example from Nord [1988] 1991:6)

Translating as a Communicative Action

We understand communication as being carried out by means of signs, which are verbal or nonverbal behaviour associated with a concept or meaning by the producer, the receiver, or both. The meaning associated with the sign need not be the same for both the producer and the receiver (cf. Vermeer 1986a:102f.). Any form of behaviour (perhaps a smile or brief silence) may be intended to have meaning X by the producer and interpreted as having meaning Y by the receiver. Even an accidental state of affairs can be interpreted as a meaningful sign, just as a sign intended to be meaningful may go unnoticed by the addressee.

The use of signs is teleological in the sense that it aims at a particular goal. In order to obtain the intended goal, the producer and the receiver must have some kind of agreement about the meaning of the sign. Signs are conventional and thus culture-specific.

Example: Germans usually find it confusing that the Greek word for 'yes' is *nai*, which sounds like the colloquial form *nee* for the German negative *nein*. To make matters worse, the Greeks seem to give an affirmative nod when they mean 'no'. Taking a closer look, however, we find that the Greek 'nod' is not exactly the same as the German one. To express agreement, a German's head bends downward from an imaginary central position, whereas the Greek negative is a slight upward jerk of the head. The example shows that we tend to interpret signs according to our own norms of behaviour.

In translation, the translator produces signs for the target audience. In order to be understood, the meaning of the signs must be known. If the translator uses signs taken from a source-culture inventory that might be misinterpreted from a target-culture point of view, it is advisable to mark the translation accordingly (see chapter 4 on documentary translation strategies).

Translating as Intercultural Action

The examples given above show that translation takes place in concrete, definable situations that involve members of different cultures. Language is an intrinsic part of a culture, especially if culture is defined as a "totality of knowledge, proficiency and perception" (Snell-Hornby 1988:40). This broad sense of the term has been made clear by the American ethnologist Ward H. Goodenough:

> As I see it, a society's culture consists of whatever it is one has to know or believe in order to operate in a manner acceptable to its members, and do so in any role that they accept for any one of themselves. Culture, being what people have to learn as distinct from their biological heritage, must consist of the end product of learning: knowledge,

in a most general, if relative, sense of the term. By this definition, we should note that culture is not a material phenomenon; it does not consist of things, people, behavior, or emotions. It is rather an organization of these things. It is the forms of things that people have in mind, their models for perceiving, relating, and otherwise interpreting them. (1964:36)

This definition has served as a general starting point for functionalist approaches to translation (Vermeer 1986a:178; Ammann 1989c:39; Nord 1993:22). Göhring (1978:10) first introduced it into the study of cross-cultural communication and slightly modified it in order to address issues of translation. Göhring stresses the fact that in intercultural encounters the individual is free either to conform to the behaviour patterns accepted in the other culture or to bear the consequences of behaviour that is contrary to cultural expectations.

In this sense, culture is a complex system. It can be subdivided into paraculture (the norms, rules and conventions valid for an entire society), diaculture (norms, rules and conventions valid for a particular group within the society, such as a club, a firm or a regional entity) and idioculture (the culture of an individual person as opposed to other individuals) (Ammann 1989c:39f).

However, the borderlines between cultural systems or sub-systems are notoriously difficult to define. A culture cannot simply be equated with a language area. For instance, the linguistic behaviour of the Scots and the English will be different in some situations and very similar in others. Or again, Dutch and Germans from the regions along their common border may differ in language but have similar value systems. In modern multicultural societies we cannot even say that a town or a street represents a single homogeneous culture. Drawing on the ideas of Michael Agar, a North American anthropologist who worked as an 'intercultural practitioner' in Mexico, I have suggested a more flexible approach (Nord 1993:20f). After a critical review of traditional anthropological definitions of culture (as those presented by Kroeber and Kluckhohn 1966 or Hofstede 1980), which saw a 'culture' as a bounded research object that was isolated in space, Agar presents a different view of culture:

Culture is something that the ICP [intercultural practitioner] creates, a story he/she tells that highlights and explains the differences that cause breakdowns. Culture is not something people *have*; it is something that fills the spaces *between* them. And culture is not an exhaustive description of anything; it focuses on differences, differences that can vary from task to task and group to group. (1992:11)

In order to emphasize the interdependence of language and culture, Agar speaks of 'languaculture' as a single entity. According to him, the culture boundary is marked by 'rich points', which are differences in behaviour causing culture conflicts or communication breakdowns between two communities in contact:

> When you encounter a new language, some things are easy to learn. You just patch on some new lexical items and grammatical forms and continue listening and talking. Other things are more difficult, but with a little effort the differences from one language to another can be bridged. But some things that come up strike you with their difficulty, their complexity, their inability to fit into the resources you use to make sense out of the world. These things – from lexical items through speech acts up to fundamental notions of how the world works – are called *rich points*. (Agar 1991:168)

This means that a translator has to be very aware of the rich points relevant to a particular translation task between the groups or sub-groups on either side of the languaculture barrier.

Translating as a Text-Processing Action

We have seen how translating is defined as translational action based on some kind of text. The expression 'some kind of text' indicates a broad concept, combining verbal and nonverbal elements, situational clues and 'hidden' or presupposed information. The proportion of verbalized to non-verbalized text elements in a particular type of situation is considered to be culture-specific. This means that while members of one culture may tend to verbalize a particular text part (for example, by saying 'Thank-you'), members of another culture may prefer to use a gesture (such as putting their hands together) or to not show any particular behaviour at all (without being regarded as impolite).

The role of the source text in functionalist approaches is radically different from earlier linguistic or equivalence-based theories. It is adequately captured by Vermeer's idea of a 'dethronement' (*Entthronung*) of the source text. The source text is no longer the first and foremost criterion for the translator's decisions; it is just one of the various sources of information used by the translator.

Like any text, a text used as a source in a translational action may be regarded as an 'offer of information' (Reiss and Vermeer 1984:72ff.). Faced with this offer, any receiver (among them, the translator) chooses the items they regard as interesting, useful or adequate to the desired purposes. In translation, the chosen informational items are then transferred to the target culture using the presentation the translator believes appropriate for the given purpose. In Vermeer's terminology, a translation is thus a new offer of information in the target culture about some information offered in the source culture and language (Reiss and Vermeer 1984:76).

Specific aspects of the role and range of source texts will be dealt with in the next chapters.

3. Basic Aspects of *Skopostheorie*

The theory of action outlined in the previous chapter provides the foundation for Hans J. Vermeer's general theory of translation, which he calls *Skopostheorie*. In addition to the works mentioned earlier (Vermeer 1978, 1983, 1986a) the theory is explained in detail in the book co-authored by Vermeer and Reiss in 1984. The first part of this book presents Vermeer's general or 'basic theory' (6-121), which is then made compatible with various translation traditions in the 'specific theories' part written by Reiss (122-219). There is nevertheless a certain discrepancy between the two parts of the book, largely due to the fact that Reiss tried to adjust her text-bound approach, originally based on equivalence theory, to Vermeer's action-oriented approach.

In the following sections we will take a closer look at some of the basic concepts presented in the book, placing particular emphasis on the relationship between the general theory (Vermeer) and the specific theories (Reiss). The first three sections will deal with Vermeer's concepts of *Skopos*, coherence and culture, while the two remaining sections explain Reiss's concepts of adequacy vs equivalence and the role of her text-typology within the frame of a functional approach to translation.

Skopos, Aim, Purpose, Intention, Function and Translation Brief

Skopos is a Greek word for 'purpose'. According to *Skopostheorie* (the theory that applies the notion of *Skopos* to translation), the prime principle determining any translation process is the purpose (*Skopos*) of the overall translational action. This fits in with intentionality being part of the very definition of any action.

To say that an action is intentional is to presuppose the existence of free will and a choice between at least two possible forms of behaviour. One form of behaviour is nevertheless held to be more appropriate than the other in order to attain the intended goal or purpose (*Skopos*). As Vermeer puts it, quoting Hubbell's translation of Cicero's *De inventione*, "genuine reasons for actions can always be formulated in terms of aims or statements of goals" (1989b:176). In his *De inventione* (2.5.18), Cicero defines actions when he speaks of cases where "some disadvantage, or some advantage is neglected in order to gain a greater advantage or avoid a greater disadvantage" (cit. Vermeer 1989b:176).

We can distinguish between three possible kinds of purpose in the field of translation: the general purpose aimed at by the translator in the translation process (perhaps 'to earn a living'), the communicative purpose aimed at by the target text in the target situation (perhaps 'to instruct the reader') and the purpose aimed at by a particular translation strategy or procedure (for example, 'to translate literally in order to show the structural particularities of the source language') (cf. Vermeer 1989a:100). Nevertheless, the term *Skopos* usually refers to the purpose of the target text.

Apart from the term *Skopos*, Vermeer uses the related words *aim*, *purpose*, *intention* and *function*. We find a distinction between *aim* and *purpose* in Vermeer 1990:93ff:

- 'Aim' (*Ziel*) is defined as the final result an agent intends to achieve by means of an action (cf. Vermeer 1986a:239). For example, a person may learn Chinese in order to read Li T'ai-po in the original (Vermeer 1989a:93).
- 'Purpose' (*Zweck*) is defined as a provisional stage in the process of attaining an aim. Aim and purpose are thus relative concepts. For example, somebody goes out to buy a Basque grammar (purpose 1) in order to learn the language (purpose 2) in order to be able to translate Basque short stories (purpose 3) in order to make Basque literature known to other language communities (aim) (example adapted from Vermeer 1989a:94).
- 'Function' (*Funktion*) refers to what a text means or is intended to mean from the receiver's point of view, whereas the *aim* is the purpose for which it is needed or supposed to be needed (cf. Vermeer 1989a:95).
- 'Intention' (*Intention* or *Absicht*) is conceived as an "aim-oriented plan of action" (Vermeer [1978] 1983:41) on the part of both the sender and the receiver, pointing toward an appropriate way of producing or understanding the text (cf. Vermeer 1986a:414). The term *intention* is also equated with *function of the action* (Reiss and Vermeer 1984:98).

In order to avoid this conceptual confusion, I have proposed a basic distinction between *intention* and *function* (Nord [1988] 1991:47f). 'Intention' is defined from the viewpoint of the sender, who wants to achieve a certain purpose with the text. Yet the best of intentions do not guarantee a perfect result, particularly in cases where the situations of the sender and the receiver differ considerably. In accordance with the model of text-bound interaction, the receivers use the text with a certain function, depending on their own expectations, needs, previous knowledge and situational conditions. In an ideal situation the sender's intention will find its aim, in which case intention and function would be analogous or even identical.

This distinction is particularly useful in translation, where the sender and receiver by definition belong to different cultural and situational settings. Because of this separation of sender and receiver, intention and function may have to be analyzed from two different angles.

Vermeer briefly discusses my distinction but does not take it up (cf. Vermeer 1989a:94f). As a general rule he considers the teleological concepts *aim, purpose, intention* and *function* to be equivalent (cf. Reiss and Vermeer 1984:96), subsuming them under the generic concept of *Skopos*.

The top-ranking rule for any translation is thus the '*Skopos* rule', which says that a translational action is determined by its *Skopos*; that is, 'the end justifies the means' (Reiss and Vermeer 1984:101). Vermeer explains the *Skopos* rule in the following way:

> Each text is produced for a given purpose and should serve this purpose. The *Skopos* rule thus reads as follows: translate/interpret/speak/ write in a way that enables your text/translation to function in the situation in which it is used and with the people who want to use it and precisely in the way they want it to function. (Vermeer 1989a:20, my translation)

Most translational actions allow a variety of *Skopoi*, which may be related to each other in a hierarchical order. The translator should be able to justify (*begründen*) their choice of a particular *Skopos* in a given translational situation.

This rule is intended to solve the eternal dilemmas of free vs faithful translation, dynamic vs formal equivalence, good interpreters vs slavish translators, and so on. It means that the *Skopos* of a particular translation task may require a 'free' *or* a 'faithful' translation, or anything between these two extremes, depending on the purpose for which the translation is needed. What it does *not* mean is that a good translation should *ipso facto* conform or adapt to target-culture behaviour or expectations, although the concept is often misunderstood in this way.

This misunderstanding may be due to a subsequent rule that, in a more sociological way, states that the *Skopos* can be described as a "variable of the receiver" (Reiss and Vermeer 1984:101). This means that the receiver, or rather the addressee, is the main factor determining the target-text *Skopos*. What it does *not* mean, however, is that this strictly excludes philological or literal or even word-for-word translations. There are many cases where relative literalism is precisely what the receiver (or the client or the user) needs, for example in the translation of a marriage certificate or driver's license, foreign legal texts for comparative purposes or direct quotations in newspaper reports. As Vermeer puts it,

> What the *Skopos* states is that one must translate, consciously and consistently, in accordance with some principle respecting the target

> text. The theory does not state what the principle is: this must be decided separately in each specific case. (1989b:182)

Now, the question is who decides what the principle is. Yet the answer is fairly obvious. As we have mentioned above, translation is normally done 'by assignment'. A client needs a text for a particular purpose and calls upon the translator for a translation, thus acting as the initiator of the translation process. In an ideal case, the client would give as many details as possible about the purpose, explaining the addressees, time, place, occasion and medium of the intended communication and the function the text is intended to have. This information would constitute an explicit translation brief (*Übersetzungsauftrag*).

Here we have to clarify a translation problem. The German word *Übersetzungsauftrag* may be translated literally as either *translation commission* or *translation assignment*. We find both terms used in works by (mostly German) functionalist translation scholars writing in English or translated into English. Vermeer (1989b) uses the term *commission*, whereas Pöchhacker (1995:34) and Kussmaul (1995:7 et passim) speak of *assignment*. Nord has even introduced a third term, *translating instructions*, "because it highlights the pedagogical aspect" ([1988] 1991:8, note 3). However, in a recent study Janet Fraser uses the term *brief* (1995:73), which seems to express very aptly what is meant by *Übersetzungsauftrag*. It implicitly compares the translator with a barrister who has received the basic information and instructions but is then free (as the responsible expert) to carry out those instructions as they see fit. In the present book we will thus use the term *translation brief* wherever appropriate.

The translation brief specifies what kind of translation is needed. This is why the initiator or the person playing the role of initiator (who might also be the translator) actually decides on the translation *Skopos*, even though the brief as such may not be explicit about the conditions.

Evidently, the *Skopos* often has to be negotiated between the client and the translator, especially when the client has only a vague or even incorrect idea of what kind of text is needed for the situation in question. Clients do not normally bother to give the translator an explicit translation brief; not being experts in intercultural communication, they often do not know that a good brief spells a better translation.

Note that the translation brief does not tell the translator *how* to go about their translating job, what translation strategy to use, or what translation type to choose. These decisions depend entirely on the translator's responsibility and competence. If the client and the translator disagree as to what kind of target text would serve the intended purpose best, the translator may either refuse the assignment (and starve) or refuse any responsibility for the function of the target text and simply do what the client asks for.

In many cases, of course, an experienced translator is able to infer the *Skopos* from the translational situation itself. As Vermeer puts it,

> unless otherwise indicated, it will be assumed in our culture that for instance a technical article about some astronomical discovery is to be translated as a technical article for astronomers [...] or if a company wants a business letter translated, the natural assumption is that the letter will be used by the company in question (and in most cases the translator will already be sufficiently familiar with the company's own in-house style, etc.). (Vermeer 1989b:183)

This is what I would call a 'conventional assignment', since it is based on the general assumption that, in a particular culture community at a given time, certain types of text are normally translated by certain types of translation. Katharina Reiss's correlation between text type and translation method (1971, 1976) is based precisely on this assumption.

This leads us to another, more specific aspect of *Skopostheorie*, namely the relationship between the source and target texts within a functionalist framework.

Intertextual and Intratextual Coherence

In terms of *Skopostheorie*, the viability of the brief depends on the circumstances of the target culture, not on the source culture. Since we have defined translation as a translational action involving a source text, the source is usually part of the brief. In terms of action theory, however, the agents (sender, receiver, initiator, translator) play the most important parts and it is problematic to speak of '*the* source text' unless we really only mean source-language words or sentence structures. The meaning or function of a text is not something inherent in the linguistic signs; it cannot simply be extracted by anyone who knows the code. A text is made meaningful by its receiver and for its receiver. Different receivers (or even the same receiver at different times) find different meanings in the same linguistic material offered by the text. We might even say that a 'text' is as many texts as there are receivers (cf. Nord 1992b:91).

This dynamic concept of text meaning and function is common enough in modern theories of literary reception (*Rezeptionsästhetik*). Vermeer sums it up by saying that any text is just an 'offer of information' (cf. Vermeer 1982) from which each receiver selects the items they find interesting and important. Applying this concept to translation, we could say that a target

31

text is an offer of information formulated by a translator in a target culture and language about an offer of information formulated by someone else in the source culture and language (cf. Reiss and Vermeer 1984:67ff).

This concept does not allow us to speak of *the* meaning of *the* source text being transferred to *the* target receivers. Guided by the translation brief, the translator selects certain items from the source-language offer of information (originally meant for source-culture addressees) and processes them in order to form a new offer of information in the target language, from which the target-culture addressees can in turn select what they consider to be meaningful in their own situation. In these terms, the translation process is irreversible.

What the translator can do, and should do, is to produce a text that is at least likely to be meaningful to target-culture receivers. In Vermeer's terms, the target text should conform to the standard of 'intratextual coherence' (Reiss and Vermeer 1984:109ff). This means the receiver should be able to understand it; it should make sense in the communicative situation and culture in which it is received (cf. Pöchhacker 1995:34). A communicative interaction can only be regarded as successful if the receivers interpret it as being sufficiently coherent with their situation. Accordingly, another important rule of *Skopostheorie*, the 'coherence rule', specifies that a translation should be acceptable in a sense that it is coherent with the receivers' situation (Reiss and Vermeer 1984:113). Being 'coherent with' is synonymous with being 'part of' the receiver's situation (cf. Vermeer [1978] 1983:54).

However, since a translation is an offer of information about a preceding offer of information, it is expected to bear some kind of relationship with the corresponding source text. Vermeer calls this relationship 'intertextual coherence' or 'fidelity'. This is postulated as a further principle, referred to as the 'fidelity rule' (Reiss and Vermeer 1984:114). Again, as in the case of the *Skopos* rule, the important point is that intertextual coherence should exist between source and target text, while the form it takes depends both on the translator's interpretation of the source text and on the translation *Skopos*. One possible kind of intertextual coherence could be a maximally faithful imitation of the source text. As Vermeer points out, this may be the form expected in literary translation:

> It might be said that the postulate of 'fidelity' to the source text requires that e.g. a news item should be translated 'as it was in the original'. But this too is a goal in itself. Indeed, it is by definition probably the goal that most literary translators traditionally set themselves. (1989b:179f)

Intertextual coherence is considered subordinate to intratextual coherence, and both are subordinate to the *Skopos* rule. If the *Skopos* requires a change of function, the standard will no longer be intertextual coherence with the source text but adequacy or appropriateness with regard to the *Skopos* (Reiss and Vermeer 1984:139). And if the *Skopos* demands intratextual *in*coherence (as in the theatre of the absurd), the standard of intratextual coherence is no longer valid.

Note that the *Skopos* concept is applicable not only to entire texts but also to text segments or 'in-texts' such as examples, footnotes or citations (Nord [1988] 1991:102). The *Skopos* or sub-*Skopos* of such smaller units may be different from that of other segments or the text as a whole.

The Concept of Culture and Culture-Specificity

Vermeer's concept of culture is based on Göhring's definition, which is in turn based on the concept cited from Goodenough in the previous chapter (cf. Vermeer 1986a:178):

> Culture is whatever one has to know, master or feel in order to judge whether or not a particular form of behaviour shown by members of a community in their various roles conforms to general expectations, and in order to behave in this community in accordance with general expectations unless one is prepared to bear the consequences of unaccepted behaviour. (Göhring 1978:10; my translation)

Vermeer places special emphasis on the following features of the definition: its dynamic qualities (focusing on human action and behaviour), its comprehensiveness (conceiving culture as a complex system determining any human action or behaviour, including language) and the fact that it may be used as a starting point for a descriptive as well as explicative or prescriptive approach to culture-specificity (cf. Vermeer 1986a:179). Vermeer's own definition focuses even more on norms and conventions as the main features of a culture. For him, a culture is

> the entire setting of norms and conventions an individual as a member of his society must know in order to be 'like everybody' – or to be able to be different from everybody. (Vermeer 1987a:28)

According to Vermeer, every cultural phenomenon is assigned a position in a complex system of values, it is 'evaluated'. And every individual is an element in a system of space-time coordinates. If this is accepted, transcultural action or communication across culture barriers has to take account of cultural differences with regard to behaviour, evaluation and communicative situations (cf. Vermeer 1990b:29).

Cultural features have been termed 'culturemes' (Vermeer 1983a:8). A cultureme is a social phenomenon of a culture X that is regarded as relevant by the members of this culture and, when compared with a corresponding social phenomenon in a culture Y, is found to be specific to culture X. 'Corresponding' here means that the two phenomena are comparable under certain definable conditions (cf. Vermeer and Witte 1990:137). For example, they may be different in form but similar in function (as in trains vs cars vs bicycles) or vice versa (for example, 'to have coffee' in England, in the morning vs 'tomar un café' in Spain, after dinner vs 'Kaffeetrinken' in Germany, in the afternoon).

A culture-specific phenomenon is thus one that is found to exist in a particular form or function in only one of the two cultures being compared. This does not mean that the phenomenon exists only in that particular culture. The same phenomenon might be observable in cultures other than the two in question.

Translating means comparing cultures. Translators interpret source-culture phenomena in the light of their own culture-specific knowledge of that culture, from either the inside or the outside, depending on whether the translation is from or into the translator's native language-and-culture. A foreign culture can only be perceived by means of comparison with our own culture, the culture of our primary enculturation (cf. Witte 1987:119). There can be no neutral standpoint for comparison. Everything we observe as being different from our own culture is, for us, specific to the other culture. The concepts of our own culture will thus be the touchstones for the perception of otherness. Further, our attention tends to focus on phenomena that are either different from our own culture (where we had expected similarity) or similar to our own culture (where difference had been expected).

If every action is to be seen in the context of a specific culture, this applies to translation as well. We may thus assume there are various culture-specific concepts of what constitutes translation or a translational action. This point will be taken up in the next chapter.

Adequacy and Equivalence

When presenting an offer of information the source-text author takes account of the presumed interests, expectations, knowledge and situational constraints of the source-culture addressees. Even if a source text is produced specifically for translation purposes it may be assumed that the author has some kind of source-culture addressees in mind, since source-culture text producers by definition lack all the necessary knowledge of the target culture. If they didn't, they would probably compose the target text themselves, in the target language (cf. Vermeer 1989b:175).

In the case of a translation, the translator is a real receiver of the source text who then proceeds to inform another audience, located in a situation under target-culture conditions, about the offer of information made by the source text. The translator offers this new audience a target text whose composition is, of course, guided by the translator's assumptions about their needs, expectations, previous knowledge, and so on. These assumptions will obviously be different from those made by the original author, because source-text addressees and target-text addressees belong to different cultures and language communities. This means the translator cannot offer the same amount and kind of information as the source-text producer. What the translator does is offer another kind of information in another form (cf. Reiss and Vermeer 1984:123).

This view of the translator's task directly challenges the traditional concept of equivalence as a constitutive feature of translation. But does it negate equivalence entirely? A certain answer may be found in the work of Reiss. After discussing several definitions of equivalence, Reiss does not completely abandon the concept; instead, she relates it to the superordinate concept of adequacy (*Adäquatheit*) (Reiss and Vermeer 1984:124ff)

We should note here that Reiss's concept of 'adequacy' is almost the opposite of other uses of the term. Toury, for instance, points out that "adherence to source norms determines a translation's *adequacy* as compared to the source text" (1995:56, emphasis in the original). He also cites the following definition by Even-Zohar:

> An adequate translation is a translation which realizes in the target language the textual relationships of a source text with no breach of its own [basic] linguistic system. (Even-Zohar 1975:43; Toury's translation)

Like *Adäquatheit* in German, *adequacy* describes a quality *with regard to* a particular standard, as in 'I hope you will prove adequate to the job'. This is the sense that Reiss makes use of. Within the framework of *Skopostheorie*, 'adequacy' refers to the qualities of a target text with regard to the translation brief: the translation should be 'adequate to' the requirements of the brief. It is a dynamic concept related to the process of translational action and referring to the "goal-oriented selection of signs that are considered appropriate for the communicative purpose defined in the translation assignment" (Reiss [1983] 1989:163).

'Equivalence', on the other hand, is a static, result-oriented concept describing a relationship of 'equal communicative value' between two texts or, on lower ranks, between words, phrases, sentences, syntactic structures and so on. In this context 'value' refers to meaning, stylistic connotations or communicative effect. Reiss ([1983] 1989:163) makes a distinction between the concept of equivalence used in comparative linguistics (which studies *langues* or language-systems) and the notion of textual equivalence used in translation studies (which focuses on *parole* or speech acts). *Parole*-orientation means the translator has to take account of the way linguistic signs are used by communicative agents in culture-bound situations. For example, equivalence at word rank does not imply textual equivalence, nor does equivalence at text rank automatically lead to lexical or syntactic equivalence. The *Skopos* of the translation determines the form of equivalence required for an adequate translation.

Example: For a word-for-word translation, where the purpose is a faithful reproduction of the words and structures of the source text, the translator chooses, one by one, the target-language words and structures correspond-ing exactly to those of the source-language with regard to meaning and, if possible, style. This is an *adequate* translation, which requires *equivalence* only on the ranks of words and syntactic structures. (cf. Reiss [1983] 1989:162)

For Reiss, the generic concept is adequacy, not equivalence. Equivalence may be one possible aim when translating but it is not held to be a transla-tion principle valid once and for all (cf. Reiss and Vermeer 1984:146f). Equivalence is by no means the kind of general normative defining quality we find expressed in definitions like Koller's:

> translation can be understood as the result of a text-reprocessing activity, by means of which a source-language text is transposed into a target-language text. Between the resulting text in L2 (the target-language text) and the source text in L1 (the source-language text) there exists a relationship which can be designated as a translational, or equivalence relation. (1995:196)

In *Skopostheorie*, equivalence means adequacy to a *Skopos* that requires that the target text serve the same communicative function or functions as the source text, thus preserving 'invariance of function between source and target text' (cf. Reiss and Vermeer 1984:140 and Vermeer's concept of fi-delity or intertextual coherence, outlined above). That is, the concept of equivalence is reduced to 'functional equivalence' on the text level of what Reiss refers to as 'communicative translation'. Reiss ([1983] 1989:166) gives the following example:

Source text: Is life worth living? - It depends upon the liver!
French translation: La vie, vaut-elle la peine? - C'est une question de foi(e)!
German translation: Ist das Leben lebenswert? - Das hängt von den Leberwerten ab.

The French and German translations can be considered functional equivalents of the English original because they are apt to fulfil the same communicative function (a play on words) in their respective culture communities. The pun is based on the structural properties of each language: homonymy in the case of *liver* in English, homophony between *foi* (faith) and *foie* (liver) in French, and similarity of form between *lebenswert* (worth living) and *Leberwerte* (liver count) in German. Equivalence here is thus not at word level.

The Role of Text Classifications

Having seen the source text 'dethroned' and regarded as a mere 'offer of information' or the translator's 'raw material' (Vermeer 1987b:541), one might be surprised to find that one of the specific theories in Reiss and Vermeer's 1984 book is Katharina Reiss's theory of text types. This has to be appreciated in connection with Reiss's concept of a specific translation type referred to as 'communicative translation', which we have just seen associated with a certain notion of equivalence.

According to Reiss, text typologies help the translator specify the appropriate hierarchy of equivalence levels needed for a particular translation *Skopos* (cf. Reiss and Vermeer 1984:156). Like several other German linguists and translation scholars, Reiss ([1977] 1989:105) distinguishes between two forms of text categorization, which are located on different levels of abstraction: on the one hand, text types (*Texttypen*) are classified according to the dominant communicative function (basically informative, expressive or operative); on the other, text genres or varieties (*Textsorten*) are classified according to linguistic characteristics or conventions (like those of reference books, lectures, satires or advertisements).

Reiss's text typology, first published in 1968-69, is based on the 'organon model' of language functions proposed by the German psychologist Karl Bühler in 1934. The typology will be briefly summarized in the following paragraphs (for more details see Nord 1996b:82ff).

In *informative* texts the main function is to inform the reader about objects and phenomena in the real world. The choice of linguistic and stylistic forms is subordinate to this function. Since the typology is assumed to be universal, this applies to both the source and the target cultures. In a translation where both the source and the target texts are of the informative type, the translator should attempt to give a correct and complete representation of the source text's content and should be guided, in terms of stylistic choices, by the dominant norms of the target language and culture. As Reiss points out in a more recent description of her typology ([1977] 1989:108), the informative type is also taken to include "purely phatic communication, where the actual information value is zero and the message is the communication process itself".

In *expressive* texts the informative aspect is complemented or even overruled by an aesthetic component. The stylistic choices made by the author contribute to the meaning of the text, producing an aesthetic effect on the reader. This effect has to be taken into account in translation. If the target text is meant to belong to the same category as the source (which, for example, is *not* the case in bilingual editions of poetry) the translator of an expressive text should attempt to produce an analogous stylistic effect. In this case, stylistic choices in translation are naturally guided by those made in the source text.

In *operative* texts both content and form are subordinate to the extralinguistic effect that the text is designed to achieve. The translating of operative texts into operative texts should be guided by the overall aim of bringing about the same reaction in the audience, although this might involve changing the content and/or stylistic features of the original.

In her first publications on text typology and translation, Reiss established a general correlation between text type and translation method. Within the framework of *Skopostheorie*, however, this correlation is restricted to the special case of functional invariance between source and target text. Nevertheless, Reiss's comments on the divergent relationships between content, form and effect in the three text types may also be useful in cases calling for functional change, since any kind of target text may be seen as representing a particular text type. Text-type classifications sharpen the translator's awareness of linguistic markers of communicative function and functional translation units.

Each text type is assumed to include various text genres, but one text genre (such as letters) does not necessarily correlate with just one text type: a love letter may be of the expressive type, a business letter would be informative, whereas a letter requesting help would belong to the operative type. Since text genres are characterized by conventional features, their classification plays an important role in functional translation. The importance of conventions will be discussed in greater detail in the next chapter.

4. Functionalism in Translator Training

Functionalist approaches have been developed with an orientation toward translator training, and this is still one of the main fields in which they are most useful. When discussing and evaluating the translations suggested by the students, teachers have always felt the need to refer to some kind of yardstick; when asked for a decision between two or more suggestions, they can rarely cope just by saying 'Well, it depends...'. Of course, teachers who have been trained as translators or who have worked in professional environments usually know that different contexts call for different translation solutions; they have an intuitive awareness of functionalism. But some kind of functionalist theory is needed if they are to pinpoint the factors determining the translator's decision in any given case.

In her translation-oriented text typology, Katharina Reiss set out from the hypothesis that the decisive factor in translation was the dominant communicative function of the source text. This could mean that any particular text, belonging to one particular text type, would allow for just one way of being translated, the 'equivalent' way. The practice of professional translating nevertheless indicates that Reiss's basic principle cannot be held up as a general rule. In view of this shortcoming, teachers might be tempted to revert to the old 'It depends...', not in all cases, but certainly in the translation of highly specialized texts.

It nevertheless seems to make more sense to use the intended communicative function of the *target* text as a guideline. We might thus say 'Let your translation decisions be guided by the function you want to achieve by means of your translation'. This has been found to be quite a useful rule in the translation process. Of course, the actual translations it leads to may not be radically new or different, since the rule can actually justify translation strategies as old as those proposed by Cicero, Jerome or Luther.

Obviously this 'function rule' cannot be used in the classroom situation unless we really understand the various factors involved. In this chapter we will thus explain what we mean by 'communicative functions' and how they can be identified in a text; we will see how translations can be classified according to the functions they are intended to carry out; and we will briefly discuss the role of norms and conventions in functional translation. After these basic considerations we will look at the practice of translator-training itself, asking how the acquisition of translational competence can be guided by means of appropriate translation briefs, source-text analysis and a systematic approach to translation problems. We will also consider what translation units the translator has to focus on. All this will enable us

to define and classify translation errors and evaluate the adequacy of translations as texts.

A Translation-Oriented Model of Text Functions

Various models of text function could serve as points of departure for
translator training. The model proposed here is meant to be no more than an
example. Its main advantages are that it is simple enough to be used in class
and it has a clear focus on translation. Our model draws on Karl Bühler's
organon model (1934), which also served as the starting point for Reiss's
text typology. Bühler proposed that there were three basic functions:
referential, expressive and 'appellative' (the use of language to make the
receiver feel or do something, corresponding to 'operative' in Reiss's
terminology). Here we will add a fourth function, which seems to be lacking
in Bühler's model: the phatic function, which we adapt from Roman
Jakobson's model of language functions (1960). These four basic types of
function can be broken down into various sub-functions. We will now briefly
define and describe these functions and sub-functions, focusing on the way
they are represented in texts and how they may concern specific translation
problems.

The Referential Function in Translation

The referential function of an utterance involves reference to the objects and
phenomena of the world or of a particular world, perhaps a fictional one. It
may be analyzed according to the nature of the object or referent concerned.
If the referent is a fact or state of things unknown to the receiver (for example, a traffic accident) the text function may consist in informing the reader;
if the referent is a language or a specific use of language, the text function
may be metalinguistic; if the referent is the correct way of handling a wash-
ing machine or of bottling fruit, the text function may be directive; if it is a
whole field that the receivers are to learn (for example, geography) the function may be didactic. Of course, this list of sub-functions cannot pretend to
be exhaustive.

Example: Directions for Bottling Fruit
1. Place clean, warm jars in a large bowl of boiling water.
2. Pack the jars firmly with fruit to the very top, tapping jars on a folded
   cloth or the palm of the hand to ensure a tight pack.
3. Fill the jars with boiling water or syrup to within 1/4 inch of the top.

The referential function is mainly expressed through the denotative value of the lexical items present in the text. Certain references are presumed to be familiar to the receivers and are thus not mentioned explicitly.

The referential function is oriented toward objects in real or fictitious worlds. To carry out the referential function, the receiver must be able to coordinate the message with their model of the particular world involved. Since world models are determined by cultural perspectives and traditions, receivers in the source culture may interpret the referential function differently to those in the target culture. This gives rise to significant translation problems.

Clearly, the referential function depends on the comprehensibility of the text. The function poses problems when source and target readers do not share the same amount of previous knowledge about the objects and phenomena referred to, as is often the case with source-culture realities or *realia*.

Example: An American journalist describes his first experience in learning Chinese as follows: "Mandarin, the dialect I'm wrestling with, has four tones. The first is spoken... with a highpitched sound. The second tone rises. *I think of calling to shore while wading into the waters of Maine.* The third tone dips and rises. The fourth is like the shuttlecock in badminton, struck midair and driven downward." (italics mine)

The sentence in italics is incomprehensible for a person who does not know that the waters of Maine are ice-cold. The description of the fourth tone is nevertheless comprehensible even for a person who does not know what a shuttlecock is because the author makes use of redundance ("struck midair and driven downward").

The Expressive Function in Translation

Unlike Reiss's text typology, where the expressive function is restricted to the aesthetic aspects of literary or poetic texts, the expressive function in my model refers to the sender's attitude toward the objects and phenomena of the world. It may be subdivided according to what is expressed. If the sender expresses individual feelings or emotions (for example, in an interjection) we may speak of an emotive sub-function; if what is expressed is an evaluation (perhaps a government decision) the sub-function will be evaluative. Another sub-function might be irony. Of course, a particular text can be designed to carry out a combination of several functions or subfunctions.

Example: In Simone de Beauvoir's title *Une mort très douce*, the adjective *douce* ('sweet') expresses an emotion experienced by the dying person. The English translation, *A Very Easy Death,* expresses a kind of evaluation,

41

perhaps as seen from a doctor's point of view. The German translation, *Ein sanfter Tod*, combines the two aspects because *sanft* might mean 'sweet' from the dying person's viewpoint and 'easy' or 'painless' from a more detached perspective.

The expressive function is sender-oriented. The sender's opinions or attitudes with regard to the referents are based on the value system assumed to be common to both sender and receiver. However, in the standard form of *intercultural* interaction the sender belongs to the source culture and the receiver belongs to the target culture. Since value systems are conditioned by cultural norms and traditions, the value system of the source-text author may be different from that of the target-culture receivers.

This means that an expressive function verbalized in the source text has to be interpreted in terms of the source-culture value system. If it is verbalized explicitly (perhaps by means of evaluative or emotive adjectives, as in 'Cats are nasty, horrible things!'), the readers will understand even when they disagree. But if the evaluation is given implicitly ('A cat was sitting on the doorstep') it may be difficult to grasp for readers who do not know on what value system the utterance is based (is a cat on the doorstep a good or a bad thing?). Many qualities have different connotations in two different cultures, as can be observed in national stereotypes. If said by a German, the sentence 'Germans are very efficient' probably expresses a positive evaluation, yet it might not be so positive if said by a Spaniard.

Example: In India if a man compares the eyes of his wife to those of a cow, he expresses admiration for their beauty. In Germany, though, a woman would not be very pleased if her husband did the same.

The Appellative Function in Translation

Directed at the receivers' sensitivity or disposition to act, the appellative function ('conative' in Jakobson's terminology) is designed to induce them to respond in a particular way. If we want to illustrate a hypothesis by an example, we appeal to the reader's previous experience or knowledge; the intended reaction would be recognition of something known. If we want to persuade someone to do something or to share a particular viewpoint, we appeal to their sensitivity, their secret desires. If we want to make someone buy a particular product, we appeal to their real or imagined needs, describing those qualities of the product that are presumed to have positive values in the receivers' value system. If we want to educate a person, we may appeal to their susceptibility to ethical and moral principles.

Direct indicators of the appellative function would be features like imperatives or rhetorical questions. Yet the function may also be achieved indirectly through linguistic or stylistic devices that point to a referential or expressive function, such as superlatives, adjectives or nouns expressing positive values. The appellative function may even operate in poetic language appealing to the reader's aesthetic sensitivity.

Example: Direct appellative function
"If you're an American living abroad and you need to keep track of your calls, you really ought to get the *AT&T Card*."

Example: Indirect appellative function
"Anthon Berg of Copenhagen, Denmark, famous chocolate makers since 1884, has built its reputation on the exclusive use of the finest raw materials available, combined with the strictest quality control and most careful packaging."

Example: Poetic appellative function
Book titles often make use of poetic means of the appellative function, as in *Hairy MacLary from Donaldson's Dairy*, or intertextual allusions, as in H. E. Bates' *Fair Stood the Wind for France* (cf. Nord 1993:171ff).

The appellative function is receiver-oriented. It's rather like a dart that has to hit the centre of the board to obtain a good score. While the source text normally appeals to a source-culture reader's susceptibility and experience, the appellative function of a translation is bound to have a different target. This means the appellative function will not work if the receiver cannot cooperate. The principle becomes particularly obvious in the case of examples, metatextual allusions, metaphors or comparisons (as in the cases of poetic appellative function given above).

Example: Touching on the difficulties he has in pronouncing Chinese words, the American journalist learning Chinese uses a comparison: "The sounds I'm supposed to say remind me of childhood games - whistling with a mouthful of saltines or reciting the Pledge of Allegiance with a jawbreaker roundly pressed against the palate."

The purpose of the text fragment in the above example is not to *inform* the readers about the games American children play but to enable the readers to imagine how the author felt in the classroom situation. The important point is that he felt *as if* he had to whistle or to recite some well-known or ceremonious text with his mouth full of something that made it difficult to do so. A target-culture reader unfamiliar with the consistency of saltines will not get this point, and a receiver who does not know the text of the 'Pledge of Allegiance' will probably not be amused.

The Phatic Function in Translation

The phatic function aims at establishing, maintaining or ending contact between sender and receiver. It relies on the conventionality of the linguistic, non-linguistic and paralinguistic means used in a particular situation, such as small talk about the weather or the conventional proverb used as an opening device or 'peg' in tourist information texts.

Example: A hotel list edited by the tourist agency of the German city of Bremen is introduced by a proverb: "Wie man sich bettet, so schläft man, sagt ein Sprichwort. Dabei wollen wir Ihnen, lieber Gast, mit dieser Hotelliste behilflich sein...". The purpose is simply to establish a good-humoured, friendly atmosphere. If the target culture has a similar proverb (as in French: "Comme on fait son lit, on se couche...") the translator may use a substitution. The English translation, however, does not really serve the intended purpose. It reads as follows: "There is proverb [!] which says: 'As you make your bed so you must lie on it'. That is why we hope that this Hotel List will be of service to you for you stay in Bremen."

Unconventionality of form strikes the eye and makes us think the author had a special reason for saying something precisely in that way. A phatic utterance meant as a mere 'offer of contact' may be interpreted as referential, expressive or even appellative if its form does not correspond to the receiver's expectation of conventional behaviour. The phatic function thus largely depends on the conventionality of its form. The more conventional the linguistic form, the less notice we take of it. The problem is that a form that is conventional in one culture may be unconventional in another.

Another feature of phatic utterances is that they often serve to define the kind of relationship holding between sender and receiver (formal/informal, symmetrical/asymmetrical). Here conventionality of form also plays an important part.

Example: Falling down through the rabbit hole, Alice imagines herself coming out on the other side of the earth and addressing an unknown lady: "Please, ma'am, is this New Zealand or Australia?" In Austria, the conventional form of address in this situation might be *"Bitte, gnädige Frau,* bin ich hier in Neuseeland oder in Australien?" or even *"Bitte, liebe Dame..."*, whereas in Germany, a little girl of Alice's age would probably not use any direct form of address at all and shift the politeness marker to an excuse + modal verb + indirect question: "Entschuldigen Sie bitte, können Sie mir sagen..." (literally, "Excuse me, please, could you tell me whether this is..."). This example shows that culture-specificity may occur even within one language area.

Except for purely phatic expressions or utterances, texts are rarely mono-functional. As a rule we find hierarchies of functions that can be identified by analyzing verbal or non-verbal function markers.

A Functional Typology of Translations

As we have seen, different communicative functions may require different translation strategies. If the purpose of the translation is to keep the function of the text invariant, function markers often have to be adapted to target-culture standards. On the other hand, source-culture function markers that are exactly reproduced in the target text might induce the target receivers to assign a different function to the target text. Where the source text is appellative, the target text may inform about an appeal; where the source text refers to something that is familiar to its readers, the target text may refer to something unfamiliar; where the source text establishes contact in a conventional way, the target text may strike the receiver as strange.

Example: Some tourist information on Munich specialities begins with a quoted proverb: 'Liebe geht durch den Magen' (literally, 'Love passes through the stomach'). By definition, such a proverb reproduces a widely known experience. The sentence thus has no informative value for German readers; it is a conventional introductory peg. In the French translation, the phatic function is turned into an informative one: "'L'amour passe par l'estomac,' affirme un proverbe allemand..." (literally, "'Love passes through the stomach,' states a German proverb"). In the Spanish and Portuguese versions, a literal translation of the German proverb is classified as "a well-known saying". This will strike Spanish and Portuguese readers as rather odd because they have never heard this saying before. The translations thus lack intratextual coherence for these receivers.

Functionalism does not mean that the waters of the Maine should generally be replaced by those of a Norwegian fjord, nor that cows' eyes should become deer's eyes or whatever the target culture's favourite animal is. Functionality simply means translators should be aware of these aspects and take them into consideration in their decisions.

The function of a translation can be analyzed from a double perspective, focusing (a) on the relationship between the target text and its audience (which can be defined in the same terms as the one holding between any original text and its readers), and (b) on the relationship between the target text and the corresponding source text. On the one hand, a translation is a text which is intended to function for the target receivers and, as such, may be intended for any communicative function. On the other, a translation is a kind of target-culture representation or substitute for a source-culture text. As such, it may carry out quite different functions with regard to the source.

A number of translation scholars have tried to systematize these considerations by establishing a typology of translations. Here I will only mention three approaches, all of which have a clear functional orientation.

Covert and Overt Translations (House 1977)

House (1977:188ff.) distinguishes between *covert* translations, in which the source-text function is kept intact or invariant so that it aspires to the status of an original in the target culture, and *overt* or marked translations, which have a second-level function in that the target receiver is not addressed directly but is made aware that the text is a translation. Subscribing to an equivalence-based concept of translation, House links her translation types to the nature of the source text (ST):

> In an overt translation, the ST is tied in a specific way to the source language community and culture; the ST is specifically directed at source language addressees but is also pointing beyond the source language community... A covert translation is thus a translation whose ST is not specifically addressed to a target culture audience, i.e. not particularly tied to the source language community and culture. (1977:189,194)

Translation Types based on Text Concepts (Reiss 1977)

Reiss ([1977] 1989:115, similarly in Reiss and Vermeer 1984:134ff) correlates text concept, translation type and translation aim. She emphasizes that any translation type (such as word-for-word translation, literal translation or learned translation) may be justified in particular circumstances for a particular translation aim, yet she does not conceal her conviction that the 'communicative-translation' type is the current ideal for translations. She thus seeks a target text whose linguistic form does not betray its translational origin and serves the same communicative purposes as the original, being at the same time its perfect equivalent syntactically, semantically and pragmatically (cf. Reiss and Vermeer 1984:135).

Reiss's view is taken up by Vermeer under the heading of 'Translation as Imitation' (Reiss and Vermeer 1984:88ff). Vermeer classifies the imitating form as the narrower concept of translation which is "conventional in our culture area today" (89f). He quotes Toury's critical comments on this phenomenon:

> But when one looks closer at the existing theories of translation, it immediately becomes evident that, more often than not, they do not simply include a notion of translatability, but actually *reduce* 'translation' to 'translatability'... Moreover, their notions are only *restricted* versions of a *general* concept of translatability because they always have some specified adequacy conditions which are *postulated* as the only *proper* ones, if not disguised as the only *possible* ones. (Toury 1980:26; emphasis in the original)

Documentary vs Instrumental Translation (Nord 1989)

Trying to combine the considerations brought forward by House and Reiss, I have presented a more elaborate translation typology based on strictly functionalist terms (see Nord 1989, less elaborately in Nord [1988] 1991:72f). This involves making a distinction between the function of the translation process and the function of the target text as the result of this process.

In this regard, we find two basic types of translation processes. The first aims at producing in the target language a kind of *document* of (certain aspects of) a communicative interaction in which a source-culture sender communicates with a source-culture audience via the source text under source-culture conditions. The second aims at producing in the target language an *instrument* for a new communicative interaction between the source-culture sender and a target-culture audience, using (certain aspects of) the source text as a model. Accordingly, we may distinguish between 'documentary' and 'instrumental' translations (Nord 1997c).

Documentary Forms of Translation

The result of a documentary translation process is a text whose main function is metatextual (House's 'secondary level' function). The target text, in this case, is a text about a text, or about one or more particular aspects of a text. There are various forms of documentary translation, all focusing on different aspects of the source text.

If a documentary translation focuses on the morphological, lexical or syntactic features of the source-language system as present in the source text, we may speak of a word-for-word or *interlinear* translation. This kind of translation is used in comparative linguistics or in language encyclopaedias, where the aim is to show the structural features of one language by means of another.

Function of translation	document of source-culture communicative interaction for target-culture readership			
Function of target text	metatextual function			
Type of translation	**DOCUMENTARY TRANSLATION**			
Form of translation	interlineal translation	literal translation	philological translation	exoticizing translation
Purpose of translation	reproduction of SL system	reproduction of SL form	reproduction of ST form + content	reproduction of ST form, content + situation
Focus of translation process	structures of SL lexis + syntax	lexical units of source text	syntactical units of source text	textual units of source text
Example	comparative linguistics	quotations in news texts	Greek and Latin classics	modern literary prose

Figure 2. Documentary Translations

Example:

Estando así en la cama, rogó a los yernos
Being so in the bed, he/she-asked (to) the sons-in-law

que le diesen cierta cantidad de dinero,
that him they-would-give certain amount of money,

lo que hicieron de buena voluntad, confiados en la herencia.
which they-did of good will, confident in the inheritance.

(adapted from *Fischer Lexicon Sprachen* 1961:255)

If a documentary translation is intended to reproduce the words of the original by adapting syntactic structures and idiomatic use of vocabulary to the norms of the target language, we may call it a *literal* or *grammar* translation. Apart from language classes, this kind of translation is often used for reported speech of foreign politicians in newspaper articles, in the translation of literal quotations in scholarly literature or, in combination with word-for-word methods, in intercultural studies referring to a language not familiar to the readers. The following example reproduces the excuse of a South African Sotho speaker who uses his left hand to pass something on to another person. In the interlinear gloss, functional items are represented by metalinguistic descriptions (1SG or 2SG = 1st/2nd person singular, NEG = negation particle).

Example:

```
Me-  m-     má   wo    abenkúm
1SG  NEG    give  2SG   left hand
I do not give (it to you) with the left hand
```

(Ameka 1994:445)

If a documentary translation reproduces the source text rather literally but adds the necessary explanations about the source culture or some peculiarities of the source language in footnotes or glossaries, we may speak of *philological* or *learned* translation. This form is used frequently in the translation of ancient texts (such as Homer), in Bible translation or in translations from distant cultures. In the following example taken from the English translation of a contemporary Indonesian novel, the names of historical personalities or realities of the source culture are explained in a glossary at the end of the book.

Example: "It's true...," my host said, surprising me with his long sigh. "I can understand why people think the way they do but in my opinion, which is one I share with the family here in Surakarta, Sultan Diponegoro was no hero."
[In the glossary:]
*Diponegoro. Javanese prince who led a five-year holy war against the Dutch between 1825 and 1830.

(Y.B. Mangunwijaya, *The Weaverbirds*, translated from the Indonesian by Thomas M. Hunter, Jakarta 1991)

If a documentary translation of a fictional text leaves the source-culture setting of the story unchanged, it might create the impression of exotic strangeness or cultural distance for the target audience. We may then speak of a *foreignizing* or *exoticizing* translation. The translation is documentary in that it changes the communicative function of the source text. What is appellative in the source text (for example, reminding the readers of their own world) becomes informative for target readers (showing what the source culture is like).

Example: If Gabriel García Márquez describes a Colombian village, which he calls Macondo, Colombian readers will be able to compare the description with their own knowledge or experience, thus detecting the author's hidden (appellative) message. The text cannot have the same function for European readers, who will read the text as a kind of information about an exotic country. That is, there is no direct communicative contact between the author and the target audience. The target audience plays the part of an observer listening to the conversation of two strange parties. This is not the translator's fault (however much some people like to call them 'traitors'); it is an inevitable feature of any literary translation.

Instrumental Forms of Translation

The result of an instrumental translation is a text that may achieve the same range of functions as an original text. If the target-text function is the same as that of the source text we can speak of an *equifunctional* translation; if there is a difference between source and target text functions we would have a *heterofunctional* translation; and if the (literary) status of the target text within the target-culture text corpus corresponds to the (literary) status the original has in the source-culture text corpus, we could talk about a *homologous* translation. We will now explain each of these three types.

Equifunctional translations are found in the area of technical texts, computer manuals and other pragmatic texts such as instructions for use, recipes, tourist information texts and information on products. These cases correspond to what Reiss calls 'communicative translation', where receivers ideally do not notice, or are not even interested in, the fact that they are reading a translation. It should be noted, however, that there is no universal rule that all technical texts *must* be translated instrumentally. Equifunctional translations often make use of standardized formulas or clichés.

Example: Equifunctional translations of orders:

Zutritt verboten!
No entry.
Défense d'entrer.
Prohibido entrar.

Function of translation	instrument for target-culture communicative interaction modelled according to source-culture communicative interaction		
Function of target text	referential/expressive/appellative/phatic function and/or subfunctions		
Type of translation	**INSTRUMENTAL TRANSLATION**		
Form of translation	equifunctional translation	heterofunctional translation	homologous translation
Purpose of translation	achieve ST functions for target audience	achieve similar functions as source text	achieve homologous effect to source text
Focus of translation	functional units of source text	transferable functions of ST	degree of ST originality
Example	instructions for use	'Gulliver's Travels' for children	poetry translated by poet

Figure 3. Instrumental translations

A *heterofunctional translation* is used if the function or functions of the original cannot be preserved as a whole or in the same hierarchy for reasons of cultural and/or temporal distance. If, for example, Jonathan Swift's *Gulliver's Travels* or Cervantes' *Don Quixote* is translated as a children's book, the satirical (appellative) function, which has become obsolete for most modern readers who do not know the original situation, is substituted in rank by the reference to an amusing fictional story in an exotic setting. Nida's 'dynamic equivalence' also changes the referential function in order to save the appellative function, as in the following example:

Example: The Austrian translator Eberhard Petschinka, who adapted John Godber's play *Bouncers* for a Vienna stage production *(The Bouncers: Die Nacht gehört uns)*, changed all the references to 'working-class Britons at play' (Godber) into references to working-class Viennese. He thus changed the referential function of the play in order to keep the appellative function the same.

In a *homologous translation* the *tertium comparationis* between the source and the target text is a certain status within a corpus or system, mostly with respect to literary or poetic texts. Here the target text might be supposed to represent the same, or a homologous, degree of originality as the original with regard to the respective culture-specific corpora of texts. This would mean, for example, that Greek hexameter is not translated by English hexameter but by blank verse or another metre as common as the hexameter verse was in ancient Greek poetry.

Homologous translations are 'semiotic transformations' for Ludskanov and 'creative transposition' in Jakobson's terms (cf. Bassnett 1991:18). They might include such things as the translation of Baudelaire's poetry by the German poet Stefan George. Although they are often excluded from the realm of 'translation proper', for functionalism they obey a specific *Skopos* and are thus just as justifiable as any other form of intercultural transfer. In this, they are like interlinear translations, which are located, as it were, at the other end of a broad scale of different relationships between source and target texts.

Example: Bassnett (1991:84ff.) reproduces a homologous translation of Catullus' Poem 13 by Ben Johnson, of which I quote the first five lines:

An invitation to dinner
Cenabis bene, mi Fabulle, apud me
paucis, si tibi di favent, diebus,
si tecum attuleris bonam atque magnam
cenam, non sine candida puella
et vino et sale et omnibus cachinnis. [...]

To night, grave sir, both my poore house, and I
doe equally desire your companie:
Not that we thinke us worthy such a ghest,
But that your worth will dignifie our fest,
With those that come; whose grace may make that seeme
Something, which, else, could hope for no esteeme. [...]

In the reception of an instrumental translation, readers are not supposed to be aware they are reading a translation at all. The form of the text is thus usually adapted to target-culture norms and conventions of text-type, genre, register and tenor.

Norms and Conventions in Functional Translation

At this point we ought to take a closer look at the role conventions play in functionalist approaches to translation. A general study of translation norms and conventions would definitely go beyond the scope of this book (for a general approach see, for example, Toury 1980 and Chesterman 1993). We will thus give no more than a brief explanation of some of the more important types of convention the translator may come across. For our purposes, conventions will be considered to be implicit or tacit non-binding regulations of behaviour, based on common knowledge and the expectation of what others expect you to expect them (etc.) to do in a certain situation (cf. Nord 1991:96).

When discussing the role of conventions in *Skopostheorie*, Reiss and Vermeer (1984:180ff.) restrict themselves to genre conventions. In my opinion, there are a number of other types of convention which have to be taken into consideration in functional translation.

Genre Conventions

Genre conventions are the result of the standardization of communication practices. As certain kinds of text are used repeatedly in certain situations with more or less the same function or functions, these texts acquire conventional forms that are sometimes even raised to the status of social norms. Genre conventions and norms thus play an important role in both text production (because authors have to comply with the conventions if they want to carry out their communicative intentions) and text reception (because receivers must infer the author's intentions from the conventional form of the text).

Example: Instruction texts like operating manuals, directions for use or recipes are characterized by certain syntactic structures. In English, the structure is the imperative (*melt the butter on a medium heat*) and in German, an infinitive (*Fischfilet säubern, säuern, salzen*). (cf. Nord [1988] 1991:19)

Reiss distinguishes between various kinds of genres that may be relevant to the translation process (Reiss and Vermeer 1984:180ff), the categories being complex, simple and complementary. In simple genres, the whole text belongs to the same text variety (such as a recipe), while complex genres may contain embedded texts that belong to a variety other than the embedding text (a novel may include a recipe or a business letter).

Example: In Lewis Carroll's *Alice in Wonderland* we find quite a few embedded texts: a nonsense riddle ("Why is a raven like a writing desk?"), an address ("Alice's Right Foot, Esq., Hearthrug, near the Fender"), the formal discourse of meetings ("I move that the meeting adjourn, for the immediate adoption of more energetic remedies") and so on.

Complementary or secondary genres are based on a primary text and may have a metatextual function. They can give information about a pre-text, as is done in reviews, summaries or abstracts, or they may have different operative functions, as in travesties or parodies.

Since genre conventions are mostly culture-specific, they play an important role in functional translation. If a target text is to be acceptable as representative of a target-culture genre, the translator has to be familiar with the conventions that the target text is to conform to. Further, in order to evaluate a source text's linguistic features in terms of conventionality or originality, the translator has to be familiar with the conventions of the genre to which the text belongs. A comparison between the conventional features of the source text and the genre conventions implied by the translation purpose may highlight the need for adaptations in the translation process.

Within the range of text-type conventions, we might perhaps also think of things like measurement conventions, formal conventions for numbering chapters or marking neologisms by italics, or conventions in graphic representations in technical texts (cf. Schmitt 1989:80ff.). These aspects can be seen in the following examples.

Example: How many bedrooms to a flat?
In Germany the size of an apartment or flat is measured by the number of rooms (excluding bathroom and kitchen). Therefore, an English *three-bedroom flat* or a Spanish *piso de tres dormitorios* would have to be called a *Vierzimmerwohnung* ('four-room flat') for German receivers (cf. Kussmaul 1995:94, who discusses the problem in terms of prototype semantics).

Example: Chapters, *Kapitel* and *capítulos*

Chapter XXIV
WHEREIN MR. PETER MAGNUS GROWS JEALOUS, AND THE MIDDLE-AGED LADY APPREHENSIVE, WHICH BRINGS THE PICKWICKIANS WITHIN THE GRASP OF THE LAW
(Charles Dickens, *The Pickwick Papers*)

12. Kapitel: Schelmuffsky, Herr von Thevenot und das Ende der Welt mitsamt einem Einschluß der Aufschluß über den Bibliotheksbeamten und seine Lebensumstände gewährt
(Werner Bergengruen, *Titulus*)

Capítulo 3
Viendo ahogarse a cuatro de mis compañeros
(Gabriel García Márquez, *Relato de un náufrago*)

Example: Neologism vs irony

In some conservative Spanish newspapers, neologisms that have not yet been accepted by the Spanish Academy of Language are marked by italics or quotation marks. If translated into a culture where the use of italics is restricted to marking irony, reproduction of these markers would cause serious communicative problems.

General Style Conventions

Other types of conventions may play a role in translation. A very important field is that of general style conventions. Even when there are similar structures available in the two languages compared, we often find there is a difference in usage due to different literary traditions and conventions as to what is considered good style (cf. Nord 1990-91:237ff for a comparison of some Spanish and German general style conventions). The analysis of parallel texts reveals that a particular grammatical function is expressed differently in source-culture and target-culture texts. The three important aspects of analysis are form, frequency and distribution.

Example: From a structural point of view, relative clauses exist in English, Spanish and German. However, we find that the form, frequency and textual distribution of relative clauses is rather different in the three languages. Where an English or Spanish text producer normally uses a relative clause, a German writer often (not always!) prefers alternative constructions, as in the following pairs:

- 'It all depends *on the tone or inflection with which* the word is spoken' vs 'Es hängt ganz *davon* ab, *in welchem Ton...* das Wort ausgesprochen wird' (indirect question in German);
- 'The *sounds I'm supposed to say* remind me of...' vs '*Wenn ich* bestimmte Laute hervorbringen soll, denke ich an...' (time phrase in German);
- 'Two of the finest *people I know*' vs 'Zwei meiner nettesten *Bekannten*' (nominal construction in German);
- 'Even *those who dislike* pontificating' vs 'Auch *wenn man nicht gern* den Schulmeister herauskehrt...' (conditional clause in German).
- 'Una *ley que prohibe* el empleo' vs 'Ein *gesetzliches Verbot....*' (adjective in German);
- 'Detergentes *que tienen* efectos cancerígenos' vs 'Reinigungsmittel *mit* krebserregender Wirkung' (prepositional phrase in German).

Similarly, English texts tend to use less relative clauses than Spanish ones, allowing the changes like the following:

* '*Esa* tarea *que nos repugna*' vs 'This *awkward* task' (nominal construction in English).

Teachers of translation mostly have to justify these general stylistic conventions by referring to their experience or native-speaker competence (cf. Berglund 1987). Large corpus-based comparative studies would provide valuable insights.

Comparative linguistics is mostly limited to studying differences in form, whereas differences in frequency and distribution would have to be analyzed on the basis of large corpora of parallel texts. Parallel texts are "linguistically independent products arising from an identical (or very similar) situation" (Snell-Hornby 1988:86); that is, they are original texts that, in two cultures, belong to the same text type and genre. Analyses of parallel texts have so far mainly focused on genre conventions: Kussmaul (1978) studies German and English academic texts; Snell-Hornby (1988:87ff) works on public signs from English-speaking and German-speaking countries; Mauranen (1993) compares English and Finnish academic rhetoric; Kussmaul (1995:76ff) analyzes German and English instruction leaflets; and I have dealt with German, English, French and Spanish titles and headings (Nord 1993, 1995a). The analysis of *general* style conventions would have to be based on corpora including various text types and genres.

Conventions of Nonverbal Behaviour

Conventions can be observed in any form of behaviour, not only verbal but also nonverbal (as in gestures) or paraverbal (as in intonation or prosody). Poyatos speaks of 'emblems':

> Besides those [non-ambiguous gestures] which become quite universal (e.g. the hitchhiking gesture, the raised middle finger as an insult), each culture possesses a rich repertoire of emblems..., quite often sharing homomorphic emblems that are actually antonyms (i.e. like cognates, e.g. the raised finger-ring gesture signifying 'Okay' in North America, money in Japan, a sexual insult in Venezuela, an emphatic conversational language marker or attention-getter in Spain). (1988:61)

It is interesting to note that there even seem to exist conventions regarding the representation of nonverbal or paraverbal behaviour in written language:

Example: I have carried out a brief study of the way paraverbal behaviour is verbalized in *Alice in Wonderland* and several translations into Spanish, Italian, German, French and Portuguese (Nord 1996d). The results show that the English original generally has an understated tone, as indicated by the fact that more than 50 per cent of the utterances are introduced simply by *to say* or by an illocutionary verb (such as *to ask* or *to remark*), without any reference to emotion or voice quality. Although the German translation by Enzensberger produces almost the same 'noise level' by keeping very close to the original, it sounds rather frosty to a German reader, who is accustomed to more variation in verb selection and for whom specific verbs (like *murmeln* or *kreischen*) usually indicate either loudness or pitch or emotional changes of voice quality. The German translation by Remané, on the other hand, sounds highly dramatic: the characters are not only murmuring, growling, shrieking, complaining, sobbing, stammering, moaning and grumbling all the time, but also 'sighing with a shiver', 'shrieking full of indignation' and 'whimpering and sobbing'.

This aspect also merits a more profound analysis and comparison of parallel texts, especially in the literary field, where one would have to consider the fact that literary texts have conventions of their own and do not simply imitate real-world behaviour.

Functional translation does not mean that source-culture conventions must be replaced by target-culture conventions in each and every translation. Depending on the translation purpose and type, the translator may opt for reproduction or adaptation. There are also translation tasks where some kinds of conventions have to be reproduced whereas others should be adjusted to target-culture standards:

Example: German pharmaceutical package inserts (PPI) are often accompanied by translations into immigrants' languages like Greek, Spanish and Italian. In these cases the macrostructural conventions of this text type are reproduced because they have to comply with the German law regulating pharmaceutical products. Stylistic and terminological conventions, however, have to be adjusted to target-culture standards in order to make the text comprehensible and acceptable for the target readers, which may be of vital importance in this case. The comparison of corresponding paragraphs from an original Spanish PPI and a PPI translated into Spanish from German shows that this requirement is not always met. The two texts refer to different pharmaceutical products that are prescribed as remedies for a blocked nose:

Translation from German:
OLYNTH
Campos de aplicación
Para el deshinchazón de la mucosa nasal en caso de: inflamaciones de la nariz y senos paranasales, constipado nasal, fiebre de heno, rinitis vasomotora, así como antes de efectuar medidas diagnósticas y terapéuticas en los meatos nasales.

Spanish original:
EGARONE
INDICACIONES.- Siempre que se desee una acción descongestiva de las vías nasales, al propio tiempo que una acción desinfectante. En especial se usará EGARONE en los resfriados nasales, rinitis, tamponamiento nasal, etc.

The translated text reproduces the nominal structures and the long sentences typical of German PPIs ("el deshinchazón de...", "antes de efectuar...") and gives literal translations of the German specialized terms ("campos de aplicación", "inflamaciones", "rinitis vasomotora", "constipado nasal") instead of using verbal structures ("siempre que se desee...") and the more common Spanish lexical items ("resfriados", "tamponamiento").

Translation Conventions

Since translation is a kind of communicative behaviour in its own right, cultures also tend to develop translation conventions. These may refer to the general concept of what a translation is or should be and what kind of relationship is expected to hold between a particular kind of source text and the corresponding target text in translation (perhaps in opposition to adaptation or version). Translation conventions can also concern the procedures used for the handling of particular translation problems below the text rank (for example, proper names, culture-bound realities or quotations). By analogy with Searle's regulative and constitutive rules (1969:31ff), the first set of conventions can be called 'constitutive' translational conventions, whereas the second set may be characterized as 'regulative' translational conventions (cf. Nord 1991:100).

Example: To gain an idea of how the concept of translation has changed over the past two hundred years, we simply have to compare the modern ideal of exoticization in literary translation with the *belles infidèles* of 18th-century France, where the ideal was to nationalize the source text.

Example: A difference in regulative conventions can be observed in the handling of proper names in translations. In Spanish translations, for example, proper names are traditionally adapted to target-culture standards as far as possible: William Shakespeare becomes *Guillermo* Shakespeare, Johann Wolfgang Goethe is transformed into *Juan Wolfgango* Goethe. In fictional texts, this means that proper names cannot be used as culture markers, unlike the situation in German literature. A German girl may be called *Federica* in a Spanish novel and her French boyfriend could be *Carlos*, regardless of the setting. In a German novel, the name *Carlos* would conventionally point to a Spanish nationality, whereas a French boyfriend could be called *Charles*.

We will come back to the problem of constitutive translation conventions in chapter 8.

Source-text Analysis, Translation Briefs & Identifying Translation Problems

Let's now look a little more closely at three aspects of functionalism that are particularly useful in translator training: the importance of the translation brief, the role of source-text analysis, and the classification and hierarchization of translation problems.

The Importance of the Translation Brief in Translator Training

If we want to turn the above considerations into tools for translator training, we clearly cannot pretend that a given source text contains all the instructions about how it should be translated. We have seen how the purpose of the target text can often be inferred from the translation situation itself, which is interpreted in accordance with the translator's previous experience or routine. Lacking this kind of experience, trainee translators cannot be expected to interpret a situation that, in the classroom, is not very clear anyway. Every translation task should thus be accompanied by a brief that defines the conditions under which the target text should carry out its particular function.

Starting from the idea that the communicative situation (including the communicators and their communicative aims) determines the verbal and nonverbal features of the text, we may assume that the description of the situational factors defines the slot into which the text should fit. This applies to both the source and target texts. The situation in which the source text fulfils its functions is, by definition, different from that of the target text. Simultaneous translation could be regarded as an exception with regard to the difference in place, time, motive and purpose of the communication, but even there we have to consider a certain difference with regard to the culture-bound knowledge, experience or susceptibility of the respective audiences. To find the aspects in which the source and the target texts will diverge, the translator has to compare the source text with the target-text profile defined in the translation brief.

The translation brief should contain (explicit or implicit) information about:

- the (intended) text function(s),
- the target-text addressee(s),
- the (prospective) time and place of text reception,
- the medium over which the text will be transmitted, and
- the motive for the production or reception of the text.

Let's look at a fairly elaborate example, which we will analyze progressively over the next few sections. Consider the following situation: For the celebration of its 600th anniversary (in 1986), the University of Heidelberg is planning an brochure that will be available in the university's main building for the whole year. Copies will be sent to other universities and institutions in Germany and abroad. The brochure is intended to inform any visitors or interested persons (also possible German sponsors and future students) about the anniversary events and further academic projects. The University Press and Information Office produces a German text for a folder with coloured photographs and an attractive layout. The text will be translated into English, French, Spanish, and Japanese; layout and photographs will be the same for all versions. Three pages of the English version of the brochure are reproduced in Figure 4 to give an impression of the layout.

This situation can be formalized as follows:

- Intended text functions: referential (information about anniversary events), appellative (image promotion, mainly by means of expressive elements);
- Addressees: visitors to Heidelberg and other people interested in the university and academic life;
- Time and place of reception: mainly Heidelberg, occasionally other places, for the whole year of the anniversary, but no longer;
- Medium: monolingual brochure with coloured photographs and short texts in a given layout;
- Reason for text production and reception: 600th anniversary of Heidelberg University.

University in the Old Town

SIXTH CENTENARY

From Tradition into the Future

"From tradition into the future" is the motto for 1986, the 600th anniversary of Heidelberg University. Its present and future role, in academic and public life, is rooted in this tradition. Forward-looking projects to mark the occasion include the Heidelberg University International Forum (a conference centre for local and visiting scholars), the construction of underground archives for valuable University Library stacks and the establishment of a computer network available to all faculties.

Events include over 100 international congresses and symposiums, concerts, theatrical performances, exhibitions, lectures and sporting functions, many in cooperation with our partner universities. Additional halls of residence are being built. A "Festschrift" in several volumes will commemorate the anniversary, along with special coins, medallions and postage stamps. Festivities will culminate in the week of 12 to 19 October, the climax being the formal ceremony on 18 October, Founders' Day.

600 YEARS
HEIDELBERG
UNIVERSITY
1386-1986

FURTHER INFORMATION

Press and Information Office, Grabengasse 1, Tel. 542310/1 Mon-Fri 9-12 am and 1-4 pm

Central Course Advice Office, Seminarstraße 2, Tel. 542307 Inquiries without previous appointment Mon-Fri 10-12 am and Thurs 2-5 pm

Foreign Students Office, Seminarstr. 2, Tel. 542336/7 Mon-Fr 10-12 am and Wed 2-4 pm

Heidelberg University, Grabengasse 1, Postfach 105760, D-6900 Heidelberg, Tel. 06221/541. Telex 461 515 unihd d

Detailed information may be obtained from university handbooks on sale in bookshops.

Art History Institute

Giant's House

Neuenheimer Feld

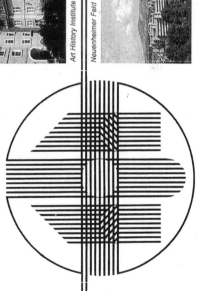

Figure 4. Heidelberg University Brochure

This information allows us to infer the following general requirements for the translations:

- In order to achieve the intended functions, the text should conform to text-type and general style conventions and a rather formal register;

- The text producer should take account of the prospective audience's culture-specific knowledge presuppositions;

- Spatial and temporal deixis will refer mainly to Heidelberg and the year of the anniversary;

- The text must fit into the space provided by the layout;

- The information on anniversary events will have priority over other data.

The Role of Source-Text Analysis

If the translation type is determined not by the source text but by the purpose of the translation process, what role does source-text analysis play in this context?

The priority of the target-text purpose does not mean the source text is completely irrelevant, as is sometimes assumed. The source text provides the offer of information that forms the starting point for the offer of information formulated in the target text. Analysis of the source text guides the translation process in that it provides the basis for decisions about (a) the feasibility of the translation assignment, (b) which source-text units are relevant to a functional translation, and (c) which translation strategy will lead to a target text meeting the requirements of the translation brief.

Various text-linguistic models can be used to analyze the source text (cf. Hönig 1986, Nord [1988] 1991). What is important, though, is that they include a pragmatic analysis of the communicative situations involved and that the same model be used for both the source text and the translation brief, thus making the results comparable. In terms of the Heidelberg University text, a comparison of the source text-in-situation with the translation brief leads to the following conclusion: the two texts differ with regard to addressee and hierarchy of text functions. In the case of the German original, the addressees are not only German-speaking visitors to Heidelberg but also potential sponsors or prospective students. This gives a higher rank to the appellative function in the German text. Even more important, however, are the differences between source-text and target-text addressees with respect to sociocultural background, world knowledge and cultural expectations.

After comparing the source text-in-situation with the target text-in-situation, the translator should be in a position to decide on optimal 'transfer' procedures:

- Comparison of the intended functions of the source and target texts leads to the conclusion that the brief can be carried out by means of a heterofunctional instrumental translation. In the target text, the information about anniversary events will have priority over the appellative-promotive function. In case of aim conflict, this aspect may justify a reduction of appellative elements in favour of informative ones.

- Comparison between source-text and target-text addressees leads to two conclusions: (a) the difference in cultural knowledge may require an adjustment of the relationship between explicit and implicit information in the text; (b) the difference in culture-specific genre expectations may require an adaptation of the text's form to target-culture textual and stylistic conventions.

- The time of reception is limited to the anniversary year for both texts. There will be no problems involving different temporal deixis.

- The occasional differences with regard to the place of reception for any receivers abroad may be ignored because these people are not the primary addressees of the text. Their interest in the University of Heidelberg may be assumed to be of a more general nature.

- The medium is the same for source and target texts. Since the target addressees' lack of source-culture knowledge may require textual expansions, the translator should be careful not to exceed the space limitations set by the layout. If any reductions prove necessary, they should not affect the anniversary information. At this point we are clearly sketching out a hierarchy of functions.

- The reason for text production and reception is the same for source and target texts. This again justifies the priority of the informative over the appellative function (further developing the hierarchy of functions).

A Systematic Approach to Translation Problems

One of the advantages of this approach to tasks in translator training (and why not in professional situations?) is that problems can be identified in advance. Note that translation *problems* are here considered to be objective or at least intersubjective; they are not to be equalled with translation *difficulties*, which are the subjective difficulties that a particular translator or trainee encounters in a translation process because of deficient linguistic, cultural or translational competence or because they do not have appropriate documentation. Translation problems will always remain problems, even when a translator has learnt how to deal with them rapidly and effectively.

The comparison between the source-text and the target-text profiles shows very clearly what source-text information or linguistic elements can be kept invariant and what has to be adjusted to the requirements of the translation purpose.

For pedagogical purposes, translation problems may be categorized as pragmatic, cultural, linguistic or text-specific. In order to apply this categorization to our sample text, here we have the first paragraph of the German original and the English, French and Spanish translations (emphases added):

Example:

(a) AUS TRADITION IN DIE ZUKUNFT
'*Aus Tradition in die Zukunft*'. So lautet das Leitmotiv des *Jubiläumsjahres* 1986, in dem die *Ruperto Carola* 600 Jahre alt wird. Im Bewußtsein ihrer jahrhundertealten Tradition formt sich ihre künftige Funktion in Wissenschaft und Gesellschaft zum Auftrag von heute. Langfristige *Jubiläumsprojekte* sind das 'Internationale *Wissenschaftsforum* Heidelberg', in dessen Rahmen Heidelberger Wissenschaftler mit auswärtigen Forschern zu Symposien zusammenkommen werden, ein *Tiefmagazin* für die wertvollen Bestände der Universitätsbibliothek und ein *Rechnernetz zur intelligenten Informationsverarbeitung* für alle Fakultäten.

(b) SIXTH CENTENARY
From Tradition into the Future
'*From tradition into the future*' is the motto for *1986, the 600th anniversary* of *Heidelberg University*. Its present and future role, in academic and public life, is rooted in this tradition. Forward-looking *projects to mark the occasion* include the Heidelberg University *International Forum* (a conference centre for local and visiting scholars), the construction of underground archives for valuable University Library stacks and the establishment of a *computer network* available to all faculties.

(c) SIX-CENTIÈME ANNIVERSAIRE
TRADITION ET MODERNISME
'*Tradition et modernisme*': C'est sous ce double signe qu'est placée l'année 1986, année du six-centième anniversaire de la fondation de l'université *Ruperto Carola*. Forte de sa tradition séculaire, Heidelberg vit déjà à l'heure du future et a choisi d'anticiper sur les tâches qui lui incomberont dans la science et la société de demain. Parmi *les projets* de longue haleine *mis en œuvre à l'occasion de cet anniversaire*, citons le *Forum International des Sciences* qui fera de Heidelberg un lieu de rencontres et d'échanges entre scientifiques de toutes nationalités, la construction d'archives souterraines destinées à abriter les trésors de la Bibliothèque Universitaire et enfin l'installation d'un *réseau informatique*.

(d) VI CENTENARIO
DESDE LA TRADICION HACIA EL FUTURO
'*Desde la tradición hacia el futuro*' es el lema bajo el que *se conmemora en 1986 el VI Centenario*. Se trata de resaltar la tradición secular de la Universidad *Ruperto Carola*. Su función actual y futura en la ciencia y en la sociedad surge como una misión que tiene su origen en esta tradición. Proyectos del VI Centenario a largo plazo son: el *Foro Científico Internacional* de Heidelberg, en el que se reunirán, en simposios, científicos de Heidelberg con investigadores de otras universidades; un almacén subterráneo para los fondos valiosos de la Biblioteca Universitaria y *una red de ordenadores para el procesamento inteligente de datos* destinada a todas las facultades.

As has been indicated above, all translation processes mediate between the source-text and target-text situations. *Pragmatic translation problems* arise from the differences between these situations and can be identified by checking on the extratextual factors (sender, receiver, medium, time, place, motive, text function). Since pragmatic translation problems are present in every translation task they can be generalized regardless of the languages and cultures involved or the direction of the translation process (into or from the native language). They are thus the most important problems to deal with in the initial phases of translator training.

Example: Receiver orientation becomes relevant in the translation of culture-bound terms, in this case the Latin name of Heidelberg University: *Ruperto Carola*. The translation of *Ruperto Carola* as 'University of Heidelberg' in the English version takes account of the fact that most English-speaking readers will not be familiar with the German habit of using Latin names for the older universities. The French and the Spanish versions could seem slightly incoherent to their readers. They might have tried to solve this problem by using 'translation couplets' (cf. Newmark 1981:31), that is, the combination of a borrowing and a target-language explanation or literal translation, although this would probably create a new pragmatic problem with regard to space limitations.

Each culture has its own habits, norms and conventions. *Cultural translation problems* are a result of the differences in the norms and conventions guiding verbal and non-verbal behaviour in the two cultures involved. They refer to all the kinds of conventions mentioned above; they are present in almost every translation task, particularly in instrumental translations. However, since they depend on the particular cultures or culture groups involved they may not have the same relevance in each case.

Example: Slogans can be regarded as forming a text type of their own, like titles and headings (cf. Nord 1993). A translation of the slogan 'Aus Tradition in die Zukunft', although it may correctly reproduce its semantic content (which is not the case in the Spanish version), will not be functional unless it sounds like a target-culture slogan. This means that it should conform to the slogan conventions of the target culture. The French version shows that this may require a complete restructuring of the source-text form.

Translation problems can also arise from structural differences in the vocabulary, syntax and suprasegmental features of the two languages. Some of these *linguistic translation problems* are restricted to language pairs, as might be the case of cognates or false friends (e.g. English *actually* vs German *aktuell*), one-to-many or one-to-zero equivalences (e.g. English *river* vs French *fleuve/rivière* and German *Berufsverbot* vs English ø). Many of these problems are nevertheless common to several or even all language pairs that include the one particular language. German modal particles, for example, cause linguistic translation problems in relation to English, Spanish, French and so on. Contrastive grammar and comparative stylistics can provide valuable help in solving these problems.

Example: A problem that often arises when working to or from German is the translation of nominal compounds such as *Jubiläumsjahr, Jubiläumsprojekte, Tiefmagazin, Rechnernetz* and *Informationsverarbeitung.* In translation teaching it is advisable to discuss the possible transfer procedures, including modulation ("se conmemora en 1986 el VI Centenario"), transposition ("1986, the 600th anniversary of Heidelberg University"), paraphrase ("projects to mark the occasion", "projets... mis en œuvre à l'occasion de cet anniversaire") or even reduction ("Rechnernetz zur intelligenten Informationsverarbeitung" vs "réseau informatique" or "computer network"). Certain reductions may be more functional in this text than a long and complicated translation of all the details (as in "una red de ordenadores para el procesamiento inteligente de datos").

Some translation problems are specifically bound to one particular source text, as may be the case for certain figures of speech, neologisms or puns. Since solutions to these text-specific problems cannot be generalized and applied to similar cases, the translator must be prepared to act creatively. However, given that our example here belongs to a rather conventional text type, it does not present any text-specific translation problems.

A Functional Hierarchy of Translation Problems

In traditional translation classes, the procedure has usually been to start from the source-language elements and transfer the text sentence by sentence or, more frequently, phrase by phrase or even, if possible, word by word. The result is a kind of draft translation whose quality may vary according to the translator's competence. This text is then polished stylistically until it seems acceptable (from the translator's personal point of view) for the communicative situation it is intended for.

This 'bottom-up' process works from the linguistic text-surface structures (stage 1) to conventions (stage 2) and finally to pragmatics (stage 3). As such, it is highly contingent on the translator's own stylistic preferences and the limitations of their linguistic and translational competence. This has several drawbacks, not only in translation practice but particularly in translation teaching.

In the bottom-up approach, translating is seen as a code-switching operation where lexical or syntactic equivalences play the most important part. Students are thus tempted to keep as close to the source-text structures as possible, which leads to linguistic interferences and mistakes even when translating into one's native language. At the same time, students often lose sight of how the text as a whole functions in its communicative situation. This leads to intuitive decisions that cannot be reasoned through intersubjectively. That is, the translator cannot really explain their decisions to the customer or revisor, nor can students and teachers really justify them to each other. Moreover, a decision taken at a lower level often has to be revised when reaching the next level. Sometimes the translation process is even blocked because of apparent untranslatability, as would be the case of the

English translator who apparently thought the proverb 'As you make your bed so you must lie on it' could adequately welcome people to a Bremen hotel.

In functional translation, problems should therefore be dealt with in a top-down way. This means that a functional translation process should start on the pragmatic level by deciding on the intended function of the translation (documentary vs instrumental). A distinction is then made between those functional elements of the source text that will have to be reproduced 'as such' and the ones that must be adapted to the addressee's background knowledge, expectations and communicative needs or to such factors as medium-restrictions and deixis requirements.

The translation type then determines whether the translated text should conform to source-culture or target-culture conventions with regard to translation style.

Only then, if at all necessary, will the differences in language system come into play. If there is still more than one possible solution at this point, the ultimate decision will be determined by contextual aspects or even, in less conventionalized or literary texts, the translator's own personal preferences, always with due respect to the function of the translation.

Applications of the model to various text types have shown there are large numbers of translation problems that can and should be dealt with in a general way in translator training. Professional training, particularly at university level, should enable trainees to acquire insights and regularities (not rules!) derived from the translation of certain sample texts and translation tasks, and then to apply those insights to any other text or translation task they may be confronted with in professional life. This can only be achieved through a systematic approach to the general problems of translation, formulated within the framework of a consistent theoretical model. The functionalist approach could provide such a framework for professional translator training.

Translation Units Revisited

The concept of 'translation units' has been a subject of debate ever since it was introduced by Vinay and Darbelnet in their *Stylistique comparée du français et de l'anglais* (1958), now almost forty years ago. Vinay and Darbelnet defined the translation unit as a *unité de pensée* linguistically materialized as "le plus petit segment de l'énoncé dont la cohésion des signes est telle qu'ils ne doivent pas être traduits séparément" ("the smallest utterance-segment in which the cohesion of the signs is such that they do not have to be translated separately"). In translation studies, there are purely linguistic approaches whose translation units range between the rank of morphemes (Diller and Kornelius 1978) or words (Albrecht 1973) or vary between phrases and sentences and the whole text in accordance with equivalence requirements (Koller 1992). We also find pragmatic approaches that include larger units like 'the complex semantic-pragmatic values of the text-type' (Neubert 1973). Bassnett and Lefevere (1990:8) even claim that the basic translation unit can be 'the culture', and they cite the example of nineteenth-century Czech literature where translations of German literary works were not intended to transfer information because everybody read German quite well anyway. In hermeneutic approaches 'the holistic effect of the text-composition' becomes a translation unit (Stolze 1982) and in psycholinguistic approaches the translation unit is determined 'intuitively' by the translator's individual translation proficiency (Königs 1981).

One might imagine that a top-down approach to translator training would want to favour the largest translation units possible. However, the larger the translation unit, the less manageable it becomes for the translator. When we get down to brass tacks, how does one actually set about translating 'the text' (apart from mini-texts like titles or road signs) or even 'the culture'? Surely by working on smaller units. Scholars interested in translator training have thus returned to smaller segments of text; for instance, Hönig (1986:243) focuses on the function a particular segment has for the overall function of the text.

All the approaches mentioned above see the translation unit, regardless of its size, as a 'horizontal' segment in the chronological sequence of linguistic elements. I have nevertheless suggested that a functionalist approach can also deal with 'vertical' units (Nord 1988, 1993, 1997b). In this view, the text is seen as a hyper-unit comprising functional units that are not rank-bound, with each unit manifested in various linguistic or non-linguistic elements that can occur at any level anywhere in the text. Let's say, for example, that the evaluative function of a text resides in a metaphor in the title + several evaluative adjectives in various sentences + a metacommunicative sentence introduced by 'I believe' + an ironic undertone accompanying the utterance + a gesture indicating contempt + the conventional structural features of a broadcasted book review. The function is thus a vertical unit bringing together all these elements.

The concept of a vertical translation unit is based on the following fundamental hypotheses from the actional concept of communication:

•   In order to give the receiver a clue as to the intended function of a particular text, senders provide their texts with markers of function or intention on various levels or ranks: textual markers refer to the overall construction of the text, structural markers refer to the order and form of paragraphs, syntactic markers refer to sentence structures and grammar, lexical markers refer to words and phrases, morphological markers to word formation, phonological markers to sound patterns, intonation, focus points, and so on.

- One particular function can be marked at various levels or ranks, and all the markers pointing to a particular function or sub-function form a functional unit. A functional unit is thus the sum of text elements or features that are intended (or interpreted as being intended) to serve the same communicative function or sub-function. If we connect these elements, we get chains or networks which, from a bird's eye view, give the impression of vertical units.
- Given the polyfunctionality of many markers, we may assume that text producers make use of marker redundancy in order to be sure the intended function is indicated clearly enough.

In a functional approach to translation, this concept has the following consequences for the definition of the translation unit:

- Communicative functions can be assumed to be universal, even though the means by which they are marked are culture-specific (they may or may not be used in the same way in both the source and the target cultures). We even come across cases of cognates, where a particular stylistic device is used to mark a particular function in the source culture but has quite different functional connotations in the target culture.
- In a given transfer situation, the professional translator analyzes the functional units of the source text and considers whether they will serve the target-text purpose. Functional units or unit-components that are used in the same way in both the source and the target cultures can be transferred to the target language as such. Functional units or components that are specific to the source culture or are used for different purposes in the target culture have to be adapted in order to meet the requirements of the target situation, unless the translation brief calls for a documentary translation, which may allow for an unchanged reproduction of source-text units. But even then, the translator has to consider the possibility that serious communicative problems could result from markers that are analogous in form but indicate different functions.

Let's look at an example. When dealing with translation units Wilss (1992:85f) claims that, from a practical point of view, the basic textual unit is the sentence, which is then divided into segments of varying size representing intuitively defined units of sense. Wilss illustrates this by translating the following fragment from a scholarly article:

Example: A nation's system of higher education / can be managed / according to two basic principles: / the manpower principle, / where the objective is / to produce the right number of persons for various professions; / and the free-choice principle, / where the objective is / to supply education / in response to the choices of the students.

Wilss's own translation of the paragraph can be divided into almost the same segments:

Das Hochschulsystem einer Nation / kann- / auf zwei Grundprinzipien / -beruhen: / dem Bedarfsprinzip, / dessen Ziel es ist, / die richtige Zahl von Absolventen für die verschiedenen akademischen Berufe zu produzieren, / und dem Wahlfreiheitsprinzip, / dessen Ziel es ist, / den Studierenden eine Hochschulausbildung nach eigener Wahl anzubieten.

A functional analysis of the text fragment could lead to the identification of the following translation units (marked by different print types):

A NATION'S SYSTEM OF HIGHER EDUCATION can be managed according to TWO BASIC PRINCIPLES: the MANPOWER PRINCIPLE, where the objective is to *produce* the *right number* of **persons** for various professions; and the FREE-CHOICE PRINCIPLE, where the objective is to *supply* education *in response to* the choices of the **students**.

(a) SMALL CAPITALS: Thematic organization. Hyper-topic: *a nation's system of higher education* - comment: *can be managed according to two basic principles*. Topic 1: *manpower principle* (+ comment: *whose objective is...*), topic 2: *free-choice principle* (+ comment: *whose objective is...*). In German, the translator should make sure the sub-themes are not presented in an inflected form ('*dem* Bedarfsprinzip' vs '*das* Bedarfsprinzip').
(b) Simple underline: Features specific to the text type. (1) Verb structures (*can be managed*, where the objective is *to produce.../to supply...*), (2) technical terms (*manpower principle, free-choice principle*). In German, features specific to the text type would include (1) a preference for nominal structures (*Organisation, Produktion, Ausbildungsangebot*), (2) analogous word formation (*Bedarfsprinzip/Optionsprinzip*), Latinisms (*Options-* instead of *Wahlfreiheits-*) and nominal compounds (*Bedarfsprinzip,Optionsprinzip,*

Berufszweige, Ausbildungsangebot), and (3) given the more complex syntactic structures of German sentences, explicit markers of thematic organization are preferred (*zum einen - zum anderen*).

(c) *Italics*: Sender-specific features. Representation of higher education as a kind of industrial production according to the laws of supply and demand (*to produce...persons, to supply education in response to...*). In the German text this aspect might be emphasized by the contrast of *Ausbildungsangebot* and *Nachfrage* and in *Produktion*, which might even by replaced by *Output* if such an emphasis on the sender's arrogant attitude can be justified by the analysis of the whole text.

(d) **Bold type**: Receiver orientation. For a translation into German we could identify an additional translation unit consisting of elements expressing receiver orientation. If the purpose of the German translation requires that the text be free of sexist language, the nouns referring to persons (*persons, students*) will form a translation unit. Wilss's translation is not consistent since he uses *Absolventen* (a generic form of the masculine gender) and *Studierende* (the non-sexist alternative to the generic masculine *Studenten*). Another problematic element for receiver orientation is the reference to *nation*. The German word *Nation* has a strong connotation of nationalism, which would be beside the point in this text. Since in the English original *a nation's* is used as a marker of generalization, it could easily be replaced in German by another marker, perhaps the plural form without an article (*Hochschulsysteme*) or the singular with an indefinite article (*ein Hochschulsystem*).

The target text resulting from this identification of functional translation units might be as follows:

Für die ORGANISATION VON **HOCHSCHULSYSTEMEN** gibt es ZWEI GRUNDPRINZIPIEN: zum einen das BEDARFSPRINZIP, bei dem der Output von genügend **Absolventinnen und Absolventen** für bestimmte Berufszweige im Vordergrund steht, und zum anderen das OPTIONSPRINZIP, bei dem sich das Ausbildungsangebot nach der Nachfrage der **Studierenden** richtet.

The analysis of functional units instead of structural units has several advantages. First, it sees the text as a complex construction in which all parts cooperate to obtain certain global purposes. That means it is indeed the *text* that is translated, and yet we do have smaller, more operable units to work on in the translation process. Second, since the linguistic or non-linguistic means of communication are rarely monofunctional, the correlation of functional units with text functions may enable us to disambiguate polyfunctional elements or use different translation techniques for the different functions of one element. Third, if various linguistic means are used to serve the same global purpose, there is no longer any need to count instances. It may be irrelevant whether the evaluative function is expressed by six or by seven adjectives. Untranslatability thereby ceases to be the translator's nightmare, because an apparently untranslatable rhetorical figure can be rendered by another device serving the same purpose, and even the omission of an untranslatable or counterproductive element becomes justifiable when the function is guaranteed by other means.

Translation Errors and Translation Evaluation

The concepts of the translation problem and the functional translation unit can also be used to define translation errors. They can also help in the evaluation of 'good' translations as being relatively 'functional' or 'adequate to the purpose'.

In foreign-language teaching a mistake or error is normally defined as a deviation from a system of norms or rules (cf. Cherubim 1980, Presch 1980). When Wilss accordingly describes a translation error as "an offence against a norm in a linguistic contact situation" ([1977] 1982:201) he is looking at translation from the point of view of foreign-language acquisition. His is not a functionalist perspective.

Translation Errors as Non-Functional Translations

For functionalism, the notion of translation error must be defined in terms of the purpose of the translation process or product. This functional perspective on errors was introduced into translation studies by Sigrid Kupsch-Losereit (1985, 1986) and further developed by Hans Hönig (1987), Paul Kussmaul (1986, 1995) and myself (Nord [1988] 1991, 1994, 1996c).

Sigrid Kupsch-Losereit defines a translation error as "an offence against: 1. the function of the translation, 2. the coherence of the text, 3. the text type or text form, 4. linguistic conventions, 5. culture- and situation-specific conventions and conditions, 6. the language system" (1985:172).

This means that a particular expression or utterance is not inadequate in itself; it only becomes inadequate with regard to the communicative function it was supposed to achieve. Inadequacy is not a quality inherent in any expression but a quality assigned to the expression from an evaluator's point of view. Even deviation from a grammatical rule may be an adequate solution in a translation intended to imitate a person's incorrect way of speaking, whereas the faithful reproduction of a factual error contained in the source text may be an inadequate translation if the target text is expected to be factually correct.

Peter A. Schmitt quotes the following excerpt from the 1983 edition of

73

the official newsletter of the German Association of Engineers (VDI):

Example: "Die 327 m lange Bundesbahn-Neubaustrecke Hannover-Würzburg... gilt als das bedeutendste Bauvorhaben der Bahn seit Gründung der Bundesrepublik Deutschland (VDI 44/83:10)." (Schmitt 1987:2)

Since the text refers to a 327 *metre* motorway going from the north of Germany to the south, anyone with a little sense of geography will realize that the distance should be 327 *kilometres*. There is no reason to reproduce the error in an instrumental translation of the text. In fact, the reproduction of this misprint could even be regarded as a translation error.

> If the purpose of a translation is to achieve a particular function for the target addressee, anything that obstructs the achievement of this purpose is a translation error.

In translator training, where we cannot expect students to have full source-language and target-language proficiency from the start, this functional definition of a translation error has several advantages. The translation brief can be formulated in such a way that the task is feasible even though there may be serious deficiencies in the students' competence. For example, if the translation brief states that the target text will be revised stylistically by a native speaker, grammatical and lexical mistakes can be tolerated to a certain degree unless they seriously block comprehension.

Further, experience shows that students make fewer linguistic mistakes if they have an exact idea of the situation for which they are translating. If they cannot imagine who is addressing whom and for what purpose, they will cling to the source-text surface structures for fear of missing the goal. Of course, the less they know about the goal, the more likely they are to miss it.

The definition of the goal is thus crucial for the evaluation of function. As we have seen, the translation brief should include explicit or implicit information on the intended functions of the target text, the addressees and, if necessary, some details on the time, place and motive of the translation's projected reception. A comparison of the translation brief with the result of source-text analysis then reveals the translation problems, be they pragmatic, cultural, linguistic or whatever. The basis for the evaluation of a translation is the adequacy or inadequacy of the solutions found for the translation problems.

Of course, solutions to translation problems are rarely a case of 'right' versus 'wrong' (Pym 1992b talks of binary and non-binary errors). Trans-

74

lation problems are usually interrelated; they form networks or hierarchies in which the solution to one problem influences the way others are tackled.

The notion of a translation problem should thus be related to that of the functional translation unit. That is, all the translation problems connected with one particular communicative function or sub-function should be solved according to a consistent strategy, which should ideally lead to the translation type required by the brief.

Let's close this section with an example:

Example: If proper names are used in a fictional text to mark the culture to which the setting belongs, all proper names form a functional translation unit. A Spanish text where the characters are called *Miguelito* and *Hugo* and which does not contain any markers of an intercultural setting is thus perfectly monocultural. In a German text, the same situation would be bicultural because *Hugo* is a German name that is not normally associated with Spain. If the translation brief requires an exoticizing documentary translation preserving the original setting, *Hugo* would have to be changed to a more typically Spanish name, perhaps *Carlos*. If the brief calls for an instrumental translation with an adaptation of the setting to the target culture (in order to allow for identification between readers and characters), *Miguelito* might have to be changed to a target-culture name, perhaps *Karlchen*. Another strategy might be to neutralize the cultural setting and use proper names common to both the source and target cultures (cf. Nord 1990-91:79ff). Without a translation brief, any of the three strategies would have to be accepted, as long as the translation is carried out consistently.

A Functional Classification of Translation Errors

If a translation error is defined as a failure to carry out the instructions implied in the translation brief and as an inadequate solution to a translation problem, then translation errors can be classified into four categories:

- Pragmatic translation errors, caused by inadequate solutions to pragmatic translation problems such as a lack of receiver orientation (as in several translations of the Heidelberg brochure analyzed above);
- Cultural translation errors, due to an inadequate decision with regard to reproduction or adaptation of culture-specific conventions (see Wilss's translation of the text on higher education, which would not be adequate as an instrumental translation);
- Linguistic translation errors, caused by an inadequate translation when the focus is on language structures (as in foreign-language classes);

- Text-specific translation errors, which are related to a text-specific translation problem and, like the corresponding translation problems, can usually be evaluated from a functional or pragmatic point of view.

A Hierarchy of Translation Errors

As in the case of translation problems, a top-down hierarchy can be drawn up for translation errors. This could be useful for grading students' work.

Experience shows that *pragmatic translation problems* are usually not very difficult to solve (once they have been identified as problems!). A bit of common sense often suffices. However, the consequences of pragmatic errors are serious, since receivers tend not to realize they are getting wrong information. Pragmatic errors are thus among the most important a translator can make. This is because the first decision in the translation process refers to the translation type best suited to the translation purpose, and each following step will be guided by this decision.

Pragmatic errors cannot be detected by looking at the target text only (for instance, by a native-speaker revisor) unless they really produce incoherence in the text. Normally they can only be identified by a person with translational competence comparing the source and target texts in the light of the translation brief.

The grading of *cultural translation errors* and *linguistic translation errors* depends on the influence they have on the function of the target text. If a missing comma or a spelling mistake leads to an inadequate interpretation of the referential function, the error is no longer a mere deviation from linguistic norms.

If the purpose of the translation task is to test language proficiency (as in foreign-language classes), linguistic errors will probably carry more weight than cultural errors. And if the purpose of the translation task is to test cultural proficiency, cultural translation problems could even be ranked higher than pragmatic errors.

Example: In the brochure published on the occasion of the 600th anniversary of Heidelberg University, the last section is on 'Further Information'. Here we find the address of the Press and Information Office, the Foreign Students Office, consulting hours, and so on. The last paragraph in the English version is: "Detailed information may be obtained from university handbooks on sale in bookshops." The Spanish version reads: "Para informaciones detalladas consultar la Guía de la Universidad, que se puede adquirir en las librerías." The English text can be interpreted correctly. The Spanish text, however, is certainly not functional with regard to receiver orientation, since there is no book called *Guía de la Universidad* on sale in Heidelberg bookshops. The French version is functional: "Pour tous renseignements précis consulter l'annuaire de l'université (*Personal- und Information-sverzeichnis*) vendu en librairie."

In a translation where the referential function is predominant, the information given in the source text would have priority over any other function or sub-function. But in a translation where the appellative function is predominant, one might be justified playing down or even omitting certain information if it obstructs the appellative function. This can be seen in the following example.

Example: A 1960s tourist leaflet about the historical town of Sagunto, near Valencia in Spain, makes much ado about the region's blast furnaces and heavy industry. In order to be functional (at least for German tourists fleeing from their industrial home regions to sunny Spain) this part of the text would require a fair amount of rewriting!

Cultural translation errors are related to the question of whether conventions should be adapted to target-culture standards. The decision depends on the previous selection of the translation type, although this does not always affect all the conventions involved in a particular communicative interaction.

Linguistic errors are often due to deficiencies in the translator's source or target-language competence. This is made clear in the following examples, which have been taken from a multilingual information leaflet distributed by the German-Spanish automobile group Volkswagen/SEAT. The leaflet advertises the company's mobile breakdown service and is handed to drivers entering Spain:

Example: SEAT Holidays in Spain
ST: Carreteras nacionales, comarcales, interiores o costeras. No importa donde vaya, los coches-taller Seat estarán allí. Todos los días. Aunque sea domingo o festivo. Y le asistirán sin cobrarle la mano de obra. Tanto si su coche es Seat, como si no. Disfrute de las vacaciones sin problemas. Los coches-taller Seat están en todas las carreteras de España.
[...]
Además la Red Seat pone a su disposición un servicio telefónico permanente. EL TELÉFONO ROJO DE LA RED SEAT.

77

TT: First and Second class highways, small interior roads or near the coast, wherever you go, the SEAT workshop-vehicles will be there. Every day. Even on Sunday or holiday. They will assist you without charging you for work. Even if your car is not a SEAT. Enjoy your leave without problems! SEAT workshop-vehicles are present on every highway in Spain!
[...]
Besides the Chain Seat put at your disposal an allday telephonic service. THE RED LINE OF THE CHAIN SEAT.

Students with inadequate proficiency in the two languages involved will not be able to focus on pragmatic or cultural translation problems in an appropriate way. Translating will then become no more than an instrument for foreign-language learning, with the focus on linguistic correctness rather than communicative or functional appropriateness. In the training of professional translators, it is thus important to make sure the trainees have acquired an adequate level of language and culture proficiency before embarking on translation exercises.

In summary, the following basic principles should be considered essential to translator training:

1. Translating without clear instructions is like swimming without water.
Language is always used within a specific situation; it is always framed by a specific sociocultural context that determines what forms of verbal and nonverbal behaviour will be regarded as appropriate by the participants. A functionally adequate translation can only be produced by someone who knows the target situation for which the text is intended and who is familiar with the communicative conventions valid in the target culture.

2. Before piloting a ship, you need some knowledge about tides and shoals and the use of life vests.
In order to keep up the motivation of the learners and to save them from unnecessary failures, a certain amount of general theoretical and methodological knowledge about the pragmatic and cultural aspects of translation should prepare them for their first practical translation exercises.

3. The most important tool for prospective translators is their own native language.
The linguistic and communicative competence of students who have just left secondary school is necessarily limited to the areas that have been present in

their lives up to then (family, school, hobbies, daily politics, sports, etc.). A professional translator nevertheless needs proficiency in other fields as well. The development of general theoretical knowledge about translation and the development of text-production skills in the native language can be combined in 'intralingual' translation exercises, i.e. rewriting texts for different audiences and purposes.

4. In order to understand the specificity of another culture, you have to know your own culture first.

We are not normally aware of how specific our way of seeing and judging the world is, nor of the non-universal ways we express our feelings and attitudes, both verbal and nonverbally. If we want to behave in an adequate way in another culture community, we have to compare the behaviour conventions of the foreign culture with those of our own. To do this, we have to replace our intuitive behaviour patterns with conscious knowledge of our own cultural specificity.

5. To use a verb in a wrong tense is less risky than to use it in the right tense at the wrong time.

People tend to have a certain natural tolerance of people who do not speak their language perfectly. They would not expect a foreigner to act according to unwritten conventions or social norms all the time; they are willing to explain their culture to foreigners or to overlook occasional mistakes. Someone who speaks the language perfectly, however, is often expected to be familiar with the conventional forms of nonverbal behaviour as well. In this case, a slight breaking of convention (perhaps arriving at eight o'clock although the invitation to 'come at eight' really meant 'come at half past eight') might have negative consequences for the social reputation of the person, who even may be considered impolite, arrogant or unreliable. Such a mistake could well be more serious than an error in language use.

5. Functionalism in Literary Translation

This chapter will deal with ways the functional approach can be applied in the translation of literary texts (cf. Nord 1988). I will first analyze the actional aspects of intracultural literary communication, trying to identify the features that distinguish literary from non-literary communication. I will then look at the *Skopos* or assignment of literary translation and the role of equivalence in this context. Using several examples taken from *Alice in Wonderland*, we will consider a few aspects of literary translation where functional perspectives may help to solve problems or to evaluate existing translations.

Actional Aspects of Literary Communication

When we analyze the agents of literary communication and the communicative situation in which literary texts occur, we find the following features:

The Sender or Author

The sender of a literary text is usually identical with the author or text-producer. Very often, the author is a person known (or presented) as a writer in the literary context of the culture community. This knowledge has a strong influence on the expectations the receivers have of the text; it may pose serious problems if the work is translated for a culture community where the author is unknown.

Intention

There can be all sorts of intentions guiding literary production. Nevertheless, in contrast to non-literary text-production, a literary author's intention is usually not to describe the 'real world' (as it is seen and acknowledged in the culture community) but to motivate personal insights about reality by describing an alternative or fictional world (cf. de Beaugrande and Dressler 1981:192). This is why literary texts are often equated with fiction. As de Beaugrande and Dressler point out, mimetic reproduction of the world is supplemented by an element of expressiveness; in Jakobson's terms, the expressive function is stronger than the referential function.

Receivers

Literary texts are primarily addressed to receivers who have specific expectations conditioned by their literary experience, as well as a certain command of the literary codes. Schmidt (1970: 65) points out that literary texts such as visual poetry can only be understood fully by readers competent in systems of interpretation by which they can make the text significant for themselves. This ability to interpret literary texts can be described as 'literary competence' (cf. de Beaugrande 1980: 22, who speaks of 'poetic competence').

Medium

In our current cultures, literary texts are mostly transmitted in writing, although orally transmitted texts such as fairy tales are included in literature as well. This may be a culture-specific feature.

Place, Time and Motive

Although the situational factors of place, time and motive may not be relevant for the distinction between literary and non-literary texts, they do play an important part in literary translation in that they convey the culture-specific features of the source and the target situations.

The Message

As has been mentioned above, literary texts usually refer to fictional objects or phenomena whose relationship with reality is not one-to-one (cf. Grabes 1977). The problem, however, is that this definition would allow any lie to be classified as a literary text, whereas a realistic or socially compromised novel could be classified as non-literary if its setting corresponds to the real world of author or readership. As de Beaugrande (1980: 29) points out,

> a fictional text [...] cannot be distinguished on the grounds that it fails to coincide with the real world; that is a property of texts in general. The main criterion is rather the extent and manner in which a text coincides with the real world, and the ways in which readers make the corresponding associations.

From a linguistic point of view, literary language has been defined as either 'deviant' from the norms of everyday communication (as in Aristotle's *Poetics* or van Dijk 1972) or as the creative use of the potential of the language system against which ordinary language use represents a reduction (cf. Coseriu 1971). Whatever stand we take on these questions of definition, literary language is clearly assumed to have a particular connotative, expressive or aesthetic meaning of its own, which may shed some light on the sender's intention or intentions (cf. Schmidt 1970a:50). The literary code includes the text conventions of traditional literary genres.

Of course, we often find literary texts that do not have any features of conventional literary style, particularly in modern literature. Such texts may reproduce slang, jargon or oral registers. In these cases the texts are paradoxically classified as literature precisely because of their lack of expected literary features.

Effect or Function

Whether literariness is seen as a particular choice of subject matter, as use of a literary code, or as a relationship with language conventions (originality vs conventionality), there is little doubt that a literary text can produce a particular aesthetic or poetic effect on its readers. This could be referred to as the specific effect or function of the literary text. It gives the literary text a specific value of its own, affecting the interaction between writer and reader. De Beaugrande (1978:20) states that

> It is the function of non-expectedness that is significant in the interaction of writer and reader, and that function may be served by ordinary as well as by non-ordinary language.

Comparing these apparently literary characteristics with the corresponding features of non-literary texts, we find that not one single factor is sufficient to define literariness on its own, since each of them can also be found in non-literary texts.

However, if we look at the fundamental importance that the sender's intention and the receiver's expectations have for the function and effect of texts, we must admit, I think, that literariness is first and foremost a pragmatic quality assigned to a particular text in the communicative situation by its users. Intratextual features are not marked 'literary' as such (they may also occur in advertisements or newspaper texts) but they do function as signals indicating the sender's literary intention to the readers. Receivers then interpret these features as literary in connection with their own culture-specific expectations, which are activated by certain extra-textual signals. The reader thus *decides* to read a text as literature. The decisive factor is that they are willing to take part in the game.

If literature must of necessity use ordinary language to create its own system, a text belonging to this system has to be marked in such a way that the reader's attention is drawn to the *extra*ordinary literary character of the text. If the text is not marked as 'literary', it may happen that the reader does not recognize its literary function, perhaps accepting its content as straight fact.

Literary markers can be set in the extratextual environment, perhaps in the inclusion of a book under the catalogue heading of 'fiction', or in the fact that a text is published in a literary magazine.

This concept of literariness depends on the culture-bound communicative intentions of both sender and receivers. It thus seems more suitable for a theory of literary translation than would be a concept based on purely linguistic features.

There remains one question that always gives rise to dispute: Can we speak of 'communicative intentions' with regard to literary texts? Some literary scholars maintain that a lack of communicative purpose is precisely one distinctive feature of literature. As far as literary translation is concerned, however, this reservation can be ignored. Even if a source text has been written without any particular purpose or intention, the translation is always addressed to some audience (however undefined it may be) and is thus intended to have some function for the readers.

If we want to identify the translation-relevant features of a literary text, we can regard literary texts as ordinary texts with a few specific features that may become important for the translator.

Let me demonstrate what I mean in a model of how literary communication might work within the framework of a particular culture C:

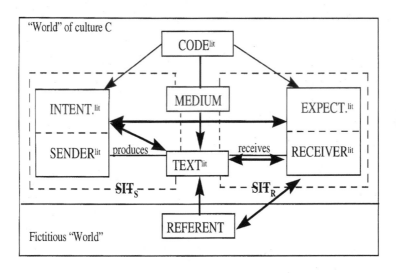

Figure 5: A Model of Literary Communication

A receiver R has specific expectations EXP determined by previous literary experience (i.e. by everything read as 'literary'). In a particular situation SIT_R (fixed with regard to time, place, motive of reception), the receiver reads (= receives) a text produced by a sender S^{lit} (who may be known as a writer in the literary context of the culture community in question) with a particular literary intention INT^{lit} in mind. The text is marked as 'literary' by an intratextual or extratextual reference to a literary code, perhaps by a poetic title or by the label 'novel' on the book cover. These markers induce the receiver to interpret the content as fictional and to interpret the sender's intention (according to given traditions of interpretation) from the stylistic and structural features of the text. Reading and interpreting the text, the receiver experiences a particular text effect. This effect may or may not be the effect intended by the sender.

The features distinguishing this communicative interaction from non-literary communication are marked ^{lit} in the diagram: the specific literary intention of the sender and the specific literary expectation of the receiver. Both are culture-bound. If the text function is mainly determined by the relation between the sender's intention and the receiver's expectation, then literariness must be basically culture-bound, regardless of any other specific function intended by the sender or a conventional function of the text type in question.

The stylistic and thematic features of the literary text TEXT^{lit} are not marked as 'literary' as such; they are interpreted as being literary on the basis of particular culture-specific signals. For this purpose, the receiver draws on individual culture-specific experience gained from the previous reading of literary texts. Under different situational conditions (perhaps a tourist brochure or a newspaper article on April Fools' Day), the same thematic and stylistic features might be interpreted as non-literary. Consequently, the specific effect of a literary text depends on both cultural and (culture-determined) individual factors.

Literary Communication across Culture Barriers

Having depicted the way literary communication might work within a single culture community, we now have to analyze how it can work across cultural and linguistic boundaries. Four basic relations contained in the model will be used to describe the crucial points of cross-cultural literary communication: (a) the relation between the sender's intention and the text, (b) the relation between the sender's intention and the receiver's expectation, (c) the relation between referent and receiver, and (d) the relation between the receiver and the text.

The Relation between the Sender's Intention and the Text

Let us assume that every author who expects their text to be read at all actually intends to produce a certain effect on the receivers and does not leave this effect to chance. The sender's intention is thus a teleological anticipation of this effect. The text producer will orient any choice of textual elements toward the intended effect. The desired effect will, in fact, only be attained if the anticipation has been adequately thought through and if the text producer is capable of verbalizing it in an appropriate way.

The text producer thus has to think about the possible effect of the text. In original literature, the sender and the text producer are one and the same person. In translated literature, however, we find split responsibilities: the sender provides the intention, and the translator tries to verbalize that intention.

As just one of many possible readers, the translator has an individual understanding of the source text and makes this the starting point for the translation (cf. Vermeer 1986d, who compares the literary translator with a conductor of an orchestra or a film director). As a rule, the translator has to infer the sender's intention from the source text, interpreting the textual features and consulting secondary sources.

In non-literary communication, the situation and the intratextual factors provide many clues about the sender's intention. This is not true in literary communication. The situation and the stylistic features of literary texts are not normally standardized. On the contrary, good literature is often described as avoiding the trodden paths of conventional expression. The code elements are often ambiguous, producing the vagueness or polysemy typical of literary texts (Schmidt 1970a:75ff.) and allowing readers a variety of interpretations. Nevertheless, there are ways and means to interpret the sender's intention, consciously or unconsciously, from the linguistic, stylistic and thematic markers in the text. Whether this interpretation actually leads to elicitation of the sender's original intention is beside the point.

Given this situation, what is actually translated is not the sender's intention but *the translator's interpretation of the sender's intention*. The target receiver, who is not always aware of reading a translated text (and does not always care much about translation in any case) may accept the translation as a manifestation of the sender's intention.

With regard to the interpretation of translated texts, we can formulate the following supposition:

Supposition 1: *The target receiver takes the translator's interpretation for the intention of the sender.*

The Relation between the Sender's Intention and the Receiver's Expectation

When producing a text, the text producer must be aware of the audience's world and cultural knowledge, their emotivity, their sociocultural environment and previous reading experience. Informational items that are supposed to belong to the receiver's horizon need not be verbalized in the text. Since a literary text does not promise any direct applicability to the real world, redundancy is less important than in pragmatic texts, where one often finds information (perhaps the necessary voltage for an electric shaver) that can be expected to be known.

An excess of presuppositions in a literary source text may present serious problems for the translator. The cultural gap between the amount of information presupposed with respect to source-text receivers and the actual cultural and world knowledge of the target-text addressees can sometime be bridged by additional information or adaptations introduced by the translator. In other cases, however, the horizons of both groups will not overlap sufficiently. The target text will then not be apt to achieve the functions intended by the source-text author, since the target receivers cannot establish coherence between their background knowledge and the information given in the text.

In the ideal case, authors anticipate their readers' background knowledge correctly and succeed in verbalizing their intention in the text. Text function and sender intention may thus be identical. In a translated text, any such identity of intention and function requires the following conditions:

- The translator has interpreted the sender's intention correctly;
- The translator succeeds in verbalizing this interpretation in such a way that it can, in turn, be interpreted correctly by the target receivers; and
- The background knowledge and expectations of the source-text addressees and the target addressees are identical or have been made to match by the translator.

With regard to the function of translated texts, this allows us to formulate a second supposition:

Supposition 2: *The function of the translated text is based on the interpretation of an interpretation of the sender's intention and on the target-cultural background knowledge and expectation of the target receivers.*

The Relation between Fiction and the Real World

As has been emphasized in chapter 2 above, the situation in which the communicative interaction takes place is part of the culture to which the sender and receiver belong. Comprehension is achieved by coordinating the information verbalized in the text with some form or manifestation of the particular model of reality stored in the receiver's mind, making the two coherent with each other. When reading a non-literary text, receivers expect the textual information to match their own model of reality. With a literary text, they nevertheless readily accept information that contrasts with their own reality (for example, trees and birds communicating with humans in a fairy tale). The greater the deviance between the reality described in the text ('text world') and the reality in which the receivers live ('reality'), the more easily the readers will accept this as a signal of literariness. What they expect in this case is not coherence between the text world and reality but coherence between the elements in the text world. If, however, the distance between the two worlds is insignificant or nonexistent, readers seem to be more likely to accept them as being identical.

In translation, this affects the target readers' comprehension of the text. The translator has to consider both the distance between the text world and source-culture reality and the distance between the text world and target-culture reality. Schematically, there are three possible varieties of cultural distance:

- The text world corresponds to source-culture reality; the source-text receivers can match it with their own world; the target receivers can't.
- The text world does not correspond to source-culture reality. Since the source-text receivers cannot coordinate it directly with their own world, the author has to give explicit descriptions of the peculiarities of the text world, which would also serve the target receivers. A special case would be a situation where the text world corresponds to the target culture. This would only pose problems of informational redundancy in the translation of non-fiction, but in literary translation it may cause serious problems for the translator if the translation is intended to transfer precisely the author's particular source-culture view of the target culture.
- The text world corresponds to source-culture reality, but is 'deculturalized' by explicit references to another (unspecific) time and/or place like 'once upon a time in a far-away land...' In this case the text world may be generalized or neutralized and the sociocultural environment loses its relevance for text reception. Source-text and target-text readers will find themselves at more or less the same distance from the text world.

The relevance of the cultural identification of the text world depends on the intended text function and effect. This applies to both the source and the target texts. The *Skopos* should then determine whether the translator leaves the text world as it is, explaining some details if necessary, or whether it is possible to neutralize or adapt the text world in order to keep the cultural distance invariant and thus achieve a particular function and effect.

With regard to the comprehension of fictional text worlds in translation, we may formulate a third supposition:

Supposition 3: *In both the source and the target situations, the comprehension of the text world depends on the cultural background and the world knowledge of the receivers.*

The Relation between the Text and the Receiver

As a rule, literary codes include not only stylistic features such as rhythm, prosody, syntax, macrostructure, metaphors and symbols but also characters, ideas, expressiveness and atmosphere. As we have seen, the relative familiarity of the text world plays an important role in achieving text effect. When readers recognize a familiar text world, they are more easily able to identify with fictional characters and situations. At the same time, critical distance is made more difficult.

In non-literary texts, language is rather conventionalized on all ranks, including macro and microstructure, syntax and morphology. In literary texts, on the other hand, the author decides which elements of the literary code should go into the text. Further, since stylistic devices are culture-bound they are not the same for the source and the target cultures, although there may well be a common ground in classical rhetorical devices. Even so, traditional stylistic features often acquire new connotations and meanings when transferred to another literary environment. This factor influences the receivers' literary background and expectations. It thus plays an important part in the attainment of literary effect.

In translation, this means that the same stylistic means can only achieve the same effect when the literary background is also the same. In other words, a translator who uses the stylistic means that the author used in the original cannot be sure the effect will be the same.

With regard to the effect of translations on their audience, we may thus formulate a fourth supposition:

Supposition 4: *The elements of the target-literature code can only achieve the same effect on their receivers as the source-literature elements have on theirs if their relation to literary tradition is the same.*

Skopos and Assignment in Literary Translation

The balance of function and effect is very delicate in cross-cultural literary communication, since it is based on a number of risky suppositions. In spite of this, literary translations are traditionally expected to begin from the concept of 'equivalence' (for a critical discussion of the concept see Snell-Hornby

1988:13ff).

In literary translation, the translator is expected to transfer not only the message of the source text but also the specific way the message is expressed in the source language (cf. Reiss 1971:42). This would ideally establish equivalence between source and target text with regard to both text function and text effect. An ideal translation would then have the same function and effect as the source text.

Yet even more demands are placed on literary translators. The translated text should be an independent, parallel work of art (cf. Fitts [1959] 1966:33) or a kind of metamorphosis of the original, able to live on in another culture (cf. Benjamin 1923). Further, the translation should reproduce the literary structure of the original (cf. Dedecius 1986:144), informing the target readers about the genre, artistic value and linguistic beauty of the original (cf. Reiss 1986:214), enriching the target language (cf. Friedrich 1965:8) and making the target readers understand why the original text was worth translating (cf. Nord 1989:55). As Reiss puts it, a literary translation

> orients itself towards the particular character of the work of art, taking as its guiding principle the author's creative will. Lexis, syntax, style and structure are manipulated in such a way that they bring about in the target language an aesthetic effect which is analogous to the expressive individual character of the source text. (1976:21; translated by Andrew Chesterman in Koller [1979] 1989:103)

All these demands can be subsumed under the concept of 'equivalence' in its widest sense. Equivalence is a normative concept. There are a number of basic requirements that must be fulfilled if the translator is to succeed in establishing equivalence between the source and the target text. In what follows I will try to match these equivalence requirements with the four suppositions formulated in the previous section.

Interpretation

Equivalence requirement 1: *The translator's interpretation should be identical with the sender's intention.*

In non-literary translation, source texts are often connected with conventional intentions: instructions for use, for example, are intended to instruct the user. The openness specific to literary texts, however, allows for various interpretations at once, making the above equivalence requirement not only impossible to meet but also rather undesirable. The complex process of text comprehension and interpretation inevitably leads to different results by different translators. To my mind, this is not at all a bad thing. Since different readers will interpret the original differently, translators should have the right to translate *their* interpretation of the text (after thorough investigation, of course). It is interesting to observe that, in history, translations based on the most personal interpretations are often the ones that become most famous.

Text Function

Equivalence requirement 2: *The translator should verbalize the sender's intention in such a way that the target text is able to achieve the same function in the target culture as that which the source text achieved in the source culture.*

This means the target text should be received as being literary within the context of the target literature. Since, as we have seen, literariness is mainly a pragmatic category, it is rather easy to fulfil this requirement by marking the target text as 'literary' externally and/or internally. Yet other source-text functions are not transferred to the target culture quite so easily. In some cases there is more than one source-text situation because the text has performed various functions at different times in history (cf. van den Broeck 1980:90f). In other cases the source-text function does simply not work with the target receivers. For example, if the author of a Latin American novel implicitly calls on the readership to change the country's autocratic system, should the translator appeal to the target audience to change their own system or the source-culture system?

Cultural Distance

Equivalence requirement 3: *The target receiver should understand the text world of the translation in the same way as the source receivers understood the text world of the original.*

This requirement can only be fulfilled when the text world is at an equal distance from both the source and the target cultures. When this is the case, all receivers can coordinate the text with their world knowledge in the same way. However, this becomes a rather illusory ideal when dealing with large language areas like Spanish in Spain and Latin America, or when dealing with older texts, because we have to ask which of the various possible source-text receivers should be taken as a model.

Text Effect

Equivalence requirement 4: *The effect the translation has on its readers should be the same as the one the source text has or had on its readers.*

We might believe that if the source text has an innovative effect because it deviates from the standards prevailing in the source-cultural literary system, the target text can only achieve an equivalent effect when it deviates to the same extent from the standards of the target-cultural literary system. Obviously, this equivalence will not be achieved through a faithful reproduction of the content and form of the original, except in the rare cases where source and target cultures have literatures that have developed more or less identically. More to the point, the effects the same text can have on various readers are so different that we can hardly speak of *the* effect of the original, even within one culture or language area.

Paradoxically, 'faithfulness' and 'equivalence' are often incompatible precisely when the source and target cultures appear to be very closely related. The smaller the cultural distance, the more likely the translator is to be trapped by cultural false friends, since everything looks so similar without really being identical. If these cultural differences are recognized and marked in the translation where necessary, the target text will no longer be a faithful reproduction of the source text but will be more likely to achieve an analogous effect.

If we now compare the equivalence requirements with our suppositions listed above, we see that the equivalence requirements are rather like a request to square the circle. We should no longer be surprised that translated literature frequently results in disappointment!

There are three possible ways out of the dilemma:

- We give up literary translation because it is impossible, perhaps telling people to learn foreign languages if they want to know foreign literatures. But exactly what is impossible here? Is it literary translation as such or just literary translation under equivalence conditions? Is equivalence a natural law, or couldn't we say it is just one possible concept of translation, a concept based on historical and cultural conventions?
- We could carry on translating as we have done up to now, following our intuition and calling the result an equivalent text, leaving the effect of the target text to the goodwill of its readers and literary critics. If translators have literary talent, they might even create literature in the process. But what about translation?
- We could try to set in place a theoretical foundation for literary translation that allows translators to justify their decisions in order to make others (translators, readers, publishers) understand what was done and why.

A functionalist approach should make the third solution viable. After all, we have seen there is actually very little difference between the communicative patterns of literary and non-literary communication.

Let me now contrast the equivalence requirements with some suggestions for a purpose-oriented approach to literary translation.

Interpretation

Skopos suggestion 1: *The translator interprets the source text not only with regard to the sender's intention but also with regard to its compatibility with the target situation.*

This means the translator compares the target text profile (time, place, motive, addressees, medium etc.) with the material offered by the source text, analyzing not only the sender's intention with regard to source-culture receivers but also the possibilities the target receivers have of coordinating the source-text information with their own situation and horizon. To do this, the translator needs as much information as possible about the intended addressees of the translation. This information must be asked from the initiator, who is often the publisher.

Text Function

Skopos suggestion 2: *The target text should be composed in such a way that it fulfils functions in the target situation that are compatible with the sender's intention.*

When analyzing the source text, the translator tries to find out which function or functions the text fulfils or has fulfilled in the source culture. The first question is which of these functions can be achieved in the target culture (and in what hierarchical order) by means of an instrumental translation, or whether a documentary translation would be more appropriate.

Cultural Distance

Skopos suggestion 3: *The text world of the translation should be selected according to the intended target-text function.*

This means there is no norm or law that says the text world has to be kept invariant in any translation. There may be cases (as in some children's books) where it is very important for the materialization of the sender's appellative intention that the target readers recognize the text world as being congruent with their own reality. In other cases, however, this recognition is not essential for the function of the text; the translation purpose may be shifted toward the reader's presumed 'interest in an exotic world', which can best be satisfied by leaving the text world as it is and explaining strange details either in the text or in footnotes, glossaries and so on.

Text Effect

Skopos suggestion 4: *The code elements should be selected in such a way that the target-text effect corresponds to the intended target-text functions.*

Like the source culture, the target culture provides linguistic means appropriate to attaining a particular text function. Using these means, the translator can be relatively sure the target receivers will recognize the intention and receive the text with the desired function. This does not mean the translator always has to adapt the text to the conventional style. Deviation from conventions also has its corresponding effects. The translator should by no means spoon-feed the target receivers. As a rule, readers do accept new, original or foreign ways of presenting old or new ideas (at least in documentary translations). This is a major way to enrich the target language by transferring unusual language use.

The translator thus has to use source-text analysis to determine whether and to what extent an imitation of the source-text style could be an appropriate way of achieving the intended function and what effect this will have (such as enrichment of target language). The result of this analysis should determine the choices made in the translation process.

Some Examples

Taking a few examples from *Alice in Wonderland* and its translations into German, French, Italian, Brazilian Portuguese and Spanish, I would like to show what the *Skopos* require-ments mean for the concrete translation process. My comments will deal with translation types, cultural distance, form and effect, fictional characters and fictional dialogues.

Choosing the Translation Type

The first example illustrates the importance of deciding on a particular translation type. Lewis Carroll uses numerous popular poems, songs and nursery rhymes, distorting them in such a way that his readers can both recognize the original and have fun reading the new version.

Example 1:

Original	Twinkle, twinkle, little bat,
	how I wonder what you're at!
	Up above the world you fly
	like a tea tray in the sky.
Model	Twinkle, twinkle, little star,
	how I wonder where you are.
	Up above the world so high
	like a diamond in the sky.

Translated by Remané

Tanze, tanze, Fledermaus,
tummle dich zum Haus hinaus.
Wie'n Tablett am Himmelszelt
fliegst du durch die weite Welt.
(no model, no notes)

Translated by Teutsch

Sah ein Knab ein Höslein stehn,
ganz aus grü-hüner Seide...
Ge-helb getupft und wu-hunderschön!
Wie kann i-hich dir wi-hiderstehn?
Du bist mei-heine Freu-heu-de!
Höslein, Höslein, Hö-höslein grün,
Mei-heine Au-haugen-wei-heide!

Model

Sah ein Knab ein Röslein stehn,
Röslein auf der Heiden,
war so jung und morgenschön,
lief er schnell es nah zu sehn,
sah's mit vielen Freuden.
Röslein, Röslein, Röslein rot,
Röslein auf der Heiden.

Translated by Ojeda

Brilla, luce, ratita alada,
¿en qué estarás tan atareada?
Por encima del Universo vuelas
como una bandeja de teteras.
Brilla, luce...

Nota (p. 203)
Esta canción es un ingenioso juego de
palabras sobre una conocida canción
infantil:

> 'Brilla, luce, pequeña estrella,
> siempre me pregunto dónde estarás,
> allá tan alta, por encima de la tierra,
> como un diamante en el firmamento.'

Translated by Bay	Brillez, brillez, petite chauve-souris! Que faites-vous si loin d'ici? Au-dessus du monde, vous planez, Dans le ciel, comme un plateau à thé Brillez, brillez... (no model, no notes)
Adapted by Cunha *de Giacomo*	Pisca, pisca, morceguinho! Voando alto ou baixinho, Que estarás fazendo au léu? Quem te vir no céu dirá Que és tal bandeja de chá Rodopiando no céu... (no model, no notes)
Translated by Bianchi	Fai l'occhietto, pipistrello! Dimmi un po' che fai di bello! Voli voli in cima al mondo, come in cielo un piatto tondo. Fai l'occhietto... (no model, no notes)

The example is taken from the chapter 'A Mad Tea Party'. After the first two lines, the Hatter asks, "You know the song perhaps?" Alice answers, "I've heard something like it."

Looking at the two German translations we find that Remané has chosen a rather literal documentary translation, whereas Teutsch used a well-known German model to play on, reproducing even the rhythm of the Mozart melody underlying Goethe's verse. Barbara Teutsch has systematically used German songs and ballads as a basis for her translations of Carroll's parodies. She told me the publisher was very reluctant to accept her translation precisely on the grounds that it did not conform to the documentary type. Yet she succeeded in the end. Personally I find that her translation really conveys the playful spirit of the original.

The Spanish translator gives a rhymed documentary translation in the text and, in a note at the end of the book, adds the English original and a rather literal translation, with a stylistic deviation (*brilla, luce* for *twinkle,*

Orig.	GermE	GermR	GermT	Italian	French	Spanish	Brazilian
Alice	Alice	Alice	Alice	Alice	Alice	Alicia	Alice
Ada	Ada	Ada	Ada	Ada	Ada	Ada	Marina
Mabel	Mabel	Mabel	Mabel	Mabel	Mabel	Mabel	Elisa
Pat	Egon	Pat	Pat	Pat	Pat	Paco	Zico
Bill	Heinz	Bill	Willi	Bill	Bill	Pepito	Bilu
Dinah	Suse	Dina	Dina	Dinah	Dinah	Dina	Mimi
Mary	Marie	Mary	Marianne	Mary	Marie	Mariana	Maria Ana
Ann	-	Ann	-	Ann	Anne	-	-
W. Rabbit	W. Kanin	W. Kanin	W. Kanin	B. Coniglio	J. Lapin	B. Conejo	Coelho
-	-	-	-	-	-	-	Branco

Figure 6. Translations of names in 'Alice in Wonderland'

twinkle) and a semantic deviation (*dónde estarás* = 'where you are', for *what you're at*). The Italian translation and the Brazilian version, which is described as an 'adaptation' on the title page, do not play on any specific existing model. Native speakers nevertheless tell me the translations sound as if they were typical children's songs. That is, in scholarly terms, they have been adapted to a kind of prototype model.

For those who criticize the adaptations as not being faithful to the original, I would like to emphasize that any documentary translation of this fragment (even those that give notes) would be fundamentally unable to establish coherence with Alice's reaction: "I've heard something like it!"

Cultural Distance

The choice of one translation type or another inevitably influences the effect the translated text will have on its readers. Cultural distance or non-distance may either add to or counteract the effect produced by the translation type.

When *Alice in Wonderland* was first published, its text world was the same as the world of the readers. This allowed for identification. For modern readers the situation is only slightly different. Although the real world of English readers has certainly changed since Lewis Carroll's time, readers for whom the book is part of the literary canon know what the original situation was like, and they have been told, where necessary, what the differences with their own situation are.

We might thus assume that English readers are still able to identify with features of this text in a variety of ways. An instrumental translation would try to make identification similarly possible for target readers, whereas a documentary translation would create foreignness and cultural distance. This distance determines the readers' reactions: the characters in the book are English; they live in England (more than 100 years ago) and it is not surprising that they live and feel and express themselves differently.

The strangeness of the text world is marked explicitly whenever the text refers to England, the English language, personalities or facts from English history. It is marked implicitly when mention is made of culture-bound realities or behavioural conventions like measures and weights. Proper names also serve as culture markers, although this function is culture-specific. In Spanish literature, for example, proper names do not always have this function (cf. Nord: 1994a).

In Figure 6 we compare the ways various translators have dealt with proper names in their translations of *Alice in Wonderland*. Note that some names, like 'Alice', are phonetically adapted in other languages. They may thus lose their function as markers of a foreign culture, even though their form has not been changed.

The names are clearly markers as to which culture the text world belongs to. The German translation by Enzensberger (GermE) presents a world in which very German characters (Heinz, Suse, Marie, Egon) live together with foreign or 'neutral' characters (Mabel, Ada, Alice). The German translation by Remané (GermR) keeps the English names (despite changing *Dinah* to *Dina* to give a more German appearance) indicating that the setting is English or at least foreign to the German reader. The German translation by Teutsch (GermT) carefully adapts the names that could look too foreign (Bill, Mary Ann, Dinah) and leaves those that could occur in German contexts, thus marking a 'German' setting. The Italian translation leaves all the names as they are; the French translation adapts only the housemaid's name (Marie-Anne); and the Brazilian version consistently marks a familiar setting. The White Rabbit's name, engraved on a brass plate at the door, is a good example of what inconsistent adaptation and invariance can do to a text. In German, it is hard to believe that a figure named 'Weißes Kaninchen' would be named 'W. Kanin' (the word *Kanin* only exists as a technical term for a rabbit's skin). In Spanish and Italian it is surprising to find a character called 'Conejo Blanco' or 'Coniglio Bianco' being named as 'B. Conejo', 'B. Coniglio', or even 'W. Coniglio' in another Italian translation. The Brazilian translator, however, uses the well-known surname combination 'Coelho Branco' to give the text a clearly familiar touch.

Form and Effect

The influence of cultural distance is felt not only with regard to the fictional information offered by the text but also with regard to the style. The effect of stylistic features depends on the extent to which they are expected by an average reader of the given text type in the given situation. Expected features give an impression of conventionality, whereas unexpected features provide an effect of originality. Thus, the translator has to opt either to 'document' the text's foreignness or to adapt it to target-culture conditions.

It is interesting to note that the equivalence concept requires invariance of content (which, as we have seen, often produces cultural distance) and, at the same time, analogous stylistic features so as to obtain equivalence of effect (cf. Reiss 1971:37ff). This means that the degree of expectedness or unexpectedness should be the same for readers of both the source text and the target text.

This problem is very clear in the field of text-type conventions. In prose literature we often find embedded texts that belong to different text types. In *Alice in Wonderland*, for example, we find a riddle, an address, a formal request proposed at a meeting, and a paragraph from a history textbook. If the translator reproduces the source-culture form of these embedded texts, the readers may not recognize the text type or could at least be surprised at the strange form given to an apparently familiar speech act.

In the following example, Alice, who has grown to more than her usual size, thinks of sending her 'poor little feet' a Christmas present:

Original	And how odd the directions will look:
	Alice's Right Foot, Esq.
	    Hearthrug,
	      near the Fender,
	        (with Alice's love).

Translated by *Teutsch*	Nur die Anschrift wird sehr komisch: Herrn Rechterfuß v. Alice z.Z. Irgendwo beim Sofa (Herzliche Grüße A.)
Translated by *Remané*	Und wie sonderbar sich die Adresse ausnehmen wird: An Seine Hochwohlgeboren den Herrn Rechten Fuß von Alice Kaminteppich Platz am Kamingitter (...Grüßen von Alice)

Adapted by
Cunha de
Giacomo
	Mandarei pelo correio, com êste enderêço:
	Pé direito de Alice.
	  Tapête perto do sofá
	   Sala de visitas
	(Com todo o carinho da Alice.)

Translated by *Bay*	Et quelle étrange addresse cela fera: Monsieur le pied droit d'Alice Tapis du Foyer Près de la Cheminée. Tendrement, Alice
Translated by *Bianchi*	E l'indirizzo sará davvero bizzarro! Preg.mo Signor

> Piede Destro de Alicis
> Tappeto Parascintille
> Caminetto
> Presso Parafuoco
> (da Alice, con affetto)

Translated by   Y en cuanto a la dirección... ¡no digamos!
Ojeda   Al Ilustrísimo Señor
                Don Pie Derecho de Alicia
                 Alfombra de la Chimenea
                     Cerca del Guardafuegos
                (Remite, con mucho afecto, Alicia)

Some translators have imitated English address conventions, including the progressive indentation of the lines, as in Ojeda's Spanish translation. Others have adapted the form to target-culture norms, as can be seen in Teutsch's German translation, which even introduces the very German abbreviation *z.Z.* (= *zur Zeit*) for a temporary address. But the layout is not the only feature that makes the text a typical address. The lines correspond to different parts of the address: complimentary forms, title, name, place, street and town. These also have standard forms in the various cultures involved and they are reproduced more or less successfully by the translators, even by those who opt for a documentary translation on other occasions.

Fictional Characters

Literary texts refer to a world in which fictional characters act and talk. Often, the characters are implicitly described by the way they talk or address each other. Indeed, this may be one of the functions of the literary text (for an analysis of paralanguage in fictional texts see Nord 1997a).

The characters' roles and relations to each other are often indicated by the forms of address, as in the following example:

Original
> The Mouse addressing Alice: 'How are you getting on now, my dear?'

Translated by Enzensberger:
> Wie fühlst du dich inzwischen, mein Kind?

Translated by Remané
> Wie fühlst du dich, meine Liebe?

Translated by Teutsch
> Nun, mein Kind, hat diese trockene Geschichte ihre Wirkung getan?

Translated by Bianchi
    Come stai adesso, bambina mia?
Adapted by Cunha de Giacomo
    Como está agora, querida?
Translated by Bay
    Comment vous sentez-vous maintenant?
Translated by Ojeda
    ¿Cómo te encuentras ahora, querida?

The forms of address characterize the speaker, the addressee, and their role-relationship. While 'my dear' is rather neutral (depending on the tone in which it is spoken), 'meine Liebe' is the form by which an elderly woman would address an equal female partner. 'Mein Kind' signals an asymmetric relationship between a superior and an inferior person, but in a friendly, familiar tone, especially when combined with the informal pronoun 'du'. In the French translation, the use of 'vous' marks a rather formal relationship. Considering that the mouse (*el ratón*) is a male character in Spanish, *querida* ('my darling') may even give the scene a slightly erotic touch.

Intonation and Focus

The importance of intonation and focus might not be obvious in written texts that are intended to be read silently. Nevertheless, sentence intonation and other prosodic elements play an important role in text function even in the written medium, although, of course, its relevance should be greater in dramatic or poetic texts.

The dialogues and narrative passages of *Alice in Wonderland* have focused words printed in italics, even though this would not have been essential for comprehensibility. Since intonation contours are rather rigid in English, these italics indicate that the main stress of the sentence (along with a raising of pitch) is on an element which would not normally be stressed in such a structural unit. The italics thus have a dramatizing function.

In German, the main stress in a sentence is indicated by a raising of pitch and intensity and may be put on any of its elements. When representing oral utterances in writing, especially in literary texts, authors can use word order or modal particles to indicate the focus points, although they more often rely on the context to suggest the right intonation.

Teutsch uses no italics at all in her translation, choosing to express focus by various other means. Her text reads quite naturally, just as if read or told by a German person. In the Spanish and French translations, most of the original's italics are reproduced; the intuitive impression is that we are listening to someone who has a strong foreign accent or is at least speaking in a very affected manner.

In Spanish, focus positions are at the beginning and end of the sentence, and the intonation contour must not be interrupted by stressed elements. There is thus no need to mark any initial or final element as being focused; italics are strictly superfluous in such cases. In other cases the focused element could easily have been placed at the end of the sentence, since the word order is relatively free.

De *buena* me he escapado esta vez!
[That *was* a narrow escape!]
'¿No terminaría *nunca* de caer?' instead of '¿No terminaría de caer nunca?'
[Would the fall *never* come to an end?]
'Nuestra familia siempre ha *odiado* a los gatos' instead of 'A los gatos, nuestra familia siempre los ha odiado.'
[Our family always *hated* cats.]

The Spanish language distinguishes between adjectives in pre-position (which cannot be focused) and adjectives in post-position (which are always focused):

...no era el momento *más oportuno*...
[this was not a *very* good opportunity for showing off her knowledge]

Spanish also has two forms of personal pronouns, one of which is reserved precisely for focused positions and does not need additional stress markers:

Pues a *ella*, naturalmente...
[Why, *she*, of course...]

In all these examples, the stress markers are strictly superfluous in Spanish and thus indicate a particular communicative intention on the part of the text producer. In other cases, however, the indicated stress is incompatible with Spanish intonation norms and produces a very unnatural way of speaking:

¡A lo mejor caiga por *toda* la tierra!
[I wonder if I shall fall right *through* the earth!]
Cuando uno se corta el dedo *muy* hondo...
[If you cut your finger *very* deeply with a knife...]

In these cases the translator could have avoided italics by using focusing involving word order or reduplication:

¡A lo mejor caiga por la tierra entera!
Cuando uno se corta el dedo muy, muy hondo...

Similar considerations apply to the French translation, where we also find a number of superfluous or even deviant italics:

Eh bien, *elle*, naturellement...
[Why, *she*, of course...]
Ce ne fût *pas du tout* le moment de...
[this was not a *very* good opportunity for showing off her knowledge]
Je me demande, continua-t-elle, si je vais *traverser* la terre.
[I wonder if I shall fall right *through* the earth!]
En tout cas, cette bouteille-là *ne* portait *pas* le mot: poison.
[However, this bottle was *not* marked 'poison'.]

We have seen how functional aspects play a role on various textual levels, from embedded text types to prosodic focus markers. We have also seen that a striving for equivalence very often leads to incoherent or inconsistent translations. This chapter was not intended to present a new theory of literary translation. Yet it should have shown that literary translation is not just an art that resists theoretical or methodological approaches. Today the conventional translation type in literary prose seems to be documentary and exoticizing, with the exception of many children's books (for example, Enid Blyton's, why?) or theatre plays (for example, Alan Ayckbourn's, why?). Readers seem to have grown accustomed to translations that are not really fun to read. As the recent debate on the German translation of Lawrence Norfolk's book *Lemprière's Dictionary* has shown (see Gerzymisch-Arbogast 1994:154f), readers are even prepared to buy millions of copies of a translation that has been publicly classified as 'problematic', to say the least, on the condition that some critics maintain the translator has done a good job of rendering the original's 'strangeness'.

As has been emphasized above, functionalism does not *a priori* advocate instrumental instead of documentary translations. Yet it can widen narrow visions, showing the possibility of a greater variety of literary translations.

6. Functionalist Approaches to Interpreting

In German translation studies, the term *Translation* (with German pronunciation) was coined by the Leipzig translation scholar Otto Kade in 1968 and has come to be widely used as a generic term covering both written and oral translation (*Übersetzen* and *Dolmetschen*). This usage reflects the idea that translating and interpreting can be regarded as 'twins' (Pöchhacker 1995:31), as two varieties of the same intercultural communicative interaction based on a source text. Note, though, that this standpoint is not shared by all scholars involved in translation and interpretation research.

In the following paragraphs we will briefly deal with the role interpreting plays in *Skopostheorie*, particularly with respect to the 'first-interpreting-then-translating' approach in translator training. We will then give a short overview of Franz Pöchhacker's recent attempt to integrate simultaneous interpretation into the general framework of translational action.

The Role of Interpreting in *Skopostheorie*

Vermeer ([1978] 1983:48) claims that since *Skopostheorie* is a *general* theory of translation, it applies to both translating and interpreting. The main difference between translating and interpreting is seen in the fact that a translation is potentially *correctable* after it is written down, whereas the result of interpreting an orally presented source text must be regarded as complete at the moment of text production. Vermeer follows Kade's definition of interpreting as

> ...the translation of a source-language text, presented only once, usually in oral form, into a target-language text which is very difficult to check and can hardly be corrected because of the lack of time. (1968: 35; my translation)

This basic non-correctability is due to certain specific conditions of text reception and production:

- In translation, the source text can be received repeatedly, as a whole or in parts; in interpreting, the source text is presented only once; the interpreter cannot receive it as a whole but only in successive parts.
- In translation, the source and the target texts remain at the translator's disposal within the translation situation; in interpreting, both texts are transitory. If an interpretation is recorded, it can be replayed only after the translational situation is finished.

- In translation, the source and the target texts are processed in a separate translation situation that is independent of the texts' communicative situations; in interpreting, the source and the target communications take place under the same situational conditions, which coincide with the translation situation (at least with regard to time; space conditions may vary, as in telephone-interpreting).

The main similarities between translating and interpreting reside in the following aspects (cf. Pöchhacker 1994a:42):

- Both interpreting and translating seek to achieve a communicative purpose (*Skopos* rule);
- The results of both activities can be defined as a target-culture offer of information about a source-culture offer of information;
- Both kinds of target text must conform to the standard of intratextual coherence (see chapter 3 above);
- Both target texts should be coherent with their respective source texts (fidelity rule).

Apart from these rather general considerations, *Skopostheorie* has not dealt with any specific aspects of the interpreting process, nor with its particular forms (consecutive interpreting, simultaneous interpreting, etc.).

Translator Training: From Interpreting to Translation

The standard curriculum for translator training in Germany follows the so-called Y-model. This means that all students receive the same initial training in language proficiency and the basics of (written) translation of general texts; after a first exam at the end of the second year they then specialize in either translation or interpreting. The two branches – translation and interpreting – are independent of each another and the final exam leads to a degree in one field or the other. A reform of this standard curriculum has been proposed by Hans J. Vermeer and Margret Ammann (1990), who have suggested an approach whose credo might be paraphrased as 'from interpreting to translation'.

In this context, interpreting does not refer to specialized professional activities like simultaneous or consecutive interpreting. The word is used in its original sense of 'making someone understand someone else's message'. So when Ammann and Vermeer say 'from interpreting to translation', they are emphasizing that any would-be translator requires the basic ability to grasp the meaning of a translation brief and retextualize a source text according to the standards of target-culture conventions. This ability is in fact 'interpreting'.

There are good reasons for privileging the place of interpreting in the training of all translators. The visibility of the situation (time, place) and the interacting persons (speaker, listeners) helps the student realize the importance of extratextual clues, which in written translation usually have to be inferred from bibliographical references or any other information available about who used the source text when and where and for what purpose. Moreover, there are many everyday situations in which interpreting takes place very naturally: going to a restaurant with a friend from abroad and interpreting the menu, helping a fellow student who does not know the language buy a train ticket, visiting a museum with a group of exchange students, and so on (see examples in chapter 2 above and Nord 1996a:321).

One of the great advantages resulting from this shift of focus is that students are made aware of the importance the communicative purpose has for any text production. Since the 'source text' is not available in written form, they are not tempted to reproduce any linguistic structures word-for-word but are instead trained to grasp the message regardless of its wording. In later phases of the training process, when they are aware that certain translation tasks require a reproduction of particular source-text features, they can be expected to have gained sufficient self-confidence to not let themselves be overwhelmed by what Wilss (1977: 206) terms the source text's "hypnotic compulsion".

A Functionalist Approach to Simultaneous Interpreting

Franz Pöchhacker is a practising conference interpreter who teaches at the University of Vienna. He has tried to integrate simultaneous conference interpreting into the framework of *Skopostheorie*, focusing on the specific aspects under which *Skopos*, intratextual coherence and culture have to be dealt with in simultaneous interpretation.

Starting from the general conceptual framework of translational action, Pöchhacker defines simultaneous interpreting as "the act of target text production in synchrony with the production and/or presentation of a source text" (1992:215). He sees the analytical key to simultaneous interpreting in the fact that the end result is ultimately shaped by the interpreter's perspective on chains of mutual assessment within the interaction network (217).

Pöchhacker's point of departure is the concept of translation as a purposeful communicative interaction taking place in a situation-in-culture. However, the relationship between the client and the interpreter is not as straightforward in interpreting as it is in written translation. The individual contributions presented by various speakers at an international conference cannot be analyzed as independent units, where each has a *Skopos* of its own; they have to be regarded as components of a greater semiotic whole, the conference itself. The conference is a kind of hypertext forming a holistic unit whose properties amount to more than the sum of its parts. In addition to the individual speeches and contributions, the interpreter has to take a large amount of non-verbal acoustic and visual information into account, including slides, overhead transparencies, handouts, and the speakers' gestures and body-language. All these factors make up the 'source text'. At the same time, the simultaneous interpreter is generally limited to verbal and paraverbal means of text production (Pöchhacker 1994:171). The people listening to the interpretation will rely on both the auditory perception of the interpreter's verbal expression, prosody, articulation, voice quality, etc. *and* the visual perception of the original speaker's gestures, facial expression, posture, and any graphic elements that the speaker may use. Technical conditions such as the interpreter's time lag may confront the target-text receiver with an asynchronous combination of auditory and visual signals (Pöchhacker 1994:172).

Pöchhacker thus situates the *Skopos* of simultaneous interpretation at the level of the conference assignment. He suggests it is not some particular target-text purpose but the conference-hypertext purpose that governs the production of functional outputs in simultaneous interpretation. The function of individual sources can be perceived as a systemic variable in the communicative interplay of speakers and listeners physically co-present at a given place and time (Pöchhacker 1995: 37).

Pöchhacker presents a multi-level analytical framework for simultaneous interpretation (1995:37). In his framework, the functional features of the text are governed by the situation, analyzed in terms of the individual interactants' roles, perceptions, dispositions and intentions, all of which form the communicative context. This text-governed-by-situation is embedded in the hypertext of the conference, whose purpose is the *Skopos* of the interpreter's action as a whole.

Pöchhacker admits that this model does not pose any serious analytical challenge to other functionalist approaches (1995:38). What might be controversial with regard to basic *Skopostheorie*, however, is the role and range of intratextual coherence and the question of how to determine which culture is determining the norms and conventions of text production in simultaneous interpretation.

As we have seen in chapter 3, 'intratextual coherence' means that the target text makes sense within the communicative situation and culture in which it is received. The coherence rule states that the translation should be coherent with or acceptable in the receiver's situation, that is, it should conform to the conventions established in the target culture for the text type in question. From a functionalist point of view, the target text in simultaneous interpreting is thus generally expected to be functionally similar to the original speech, mostly of the instrumental translation type (see chapter 4 above). As Pöchhacker puts it,

> On the general assumption that a given culture is essentially different from, rather than similar to, another culture, the target text in SI [= simultaneous interpreting] will have to be adapted to the communicative patterns and text-type conventions (expectancy norms) generally accepted for native texts in the culture in question. (1995:39)

The real problem is now what 'the culture in question' is. The use of English at international conferences as the *lingua franca* between participants from all kinds of backgrounds makes the notion of cultural transfer difficult to apply. Pöchhacker suggests drawing on Vermeer's concept of diaculture (1986a): a group culture defined by the shared professional background, common technical expertise and a history of interaction as members of a particular professional organization (cf. Pöchhacker 1995:49). This expert culture transcends national or language-cultural borderlines. The cultural differences embodied in the languages used are still there, but they are not as relevant to the process of transcultural communication as is the common ground of what the participants know and do.

Of course, the co-presence of source-language nonverbal and target-language verbal signs may produce a multimedial and bi-cultural mix (Pöchhacker 1994:178), perhaps of a kind that would lead to communication breakdown in other circumstances. Yet in the conference situation, the common diacultural ground will in most cases enable the participants to communicate successfully.

Pöchhacker's approach, which is based on a large corpus of authentic conference material, gives ample evidence that the functional approach can be applied to simultaneous interpreting. His findings must be regarded as a valuable point of departure for the evaluation of interpreters' outputs, as well as for interpreter training. More important, his studies show there is still much research to be done in this field. As Pöchhacker says, "interpreting researchers can find many exciting new challenges by taking a product-oriented approach to an interpreter's output as text-in-situation-&-culture" (1995:33).

7. Criticisms

Criticisms have been levelled at the theoretical foundations and applicability of functionalist approaches in general and of *Skopostheorie* in particular. Although, as Toury recently pointed out with reference to both *Skopostheorie* and his own target-oriented approach, "target-orientedness as such no longer arouses the same antagonism it used to less than twenty years ago" (1995:25), the ten basic criticisms discussed in this chapter are still explicitly or implicitly present in debates on translation theory in the 1990s. With regard to functionalism's theoretical foundations, critics have questioned the concepts of intentionality (Criticism 1), translation purpose, and receiver-orientation (Criticism 2), and culture-specificity (Criticism 10). The applicability of functionalism has raised criticisms with respect to the role of the translator (Criticism 6), the status of the original (Criticism 7), the role of adaptation in functional translation (Criticism 8) and the appropriateness of the concept to the translation of literary texts (Criticism 9). There have also been criticisms of a more general or meta-theoretical nature, such as the claim that functionalism stretches the concept of translation too far (Criticism 3), that it is not an original theory (Criticism 4) or that it is prescriptive and not empirical and therefore does not deserve to be called a translation theory (Criticism 5). Not all of these criticisms have been brought forward explicitly by particular scholars or schools of thought; some of them are reservations that can be inferred from what scholars or representatives of other groups say about 'modern translation theory' in general, or at least 'modern German translation theory', implicitly referring to functionalist approaches. Note, though, that functionalism cannot be equalled with anything like modern translation theory as such, not even if limited to Germany or German-speaking countries.

In the following pages I will outline each of these criticisms and answer them from the point of view of *Skopostheorie* and related functional approaches (particularly my own 'function plus loyalty' model, described in the next chapter). The order in which the criticisms will be dealt with tries to show their interrelatedness and their embedding within general misconceptions or misunderstandings of the basic claims of functionalism.

Criticism 1: Not all actions have an intention.

Some critics question the very essence of action-based translation theories. They claim there are actions that do not have any intention or purpose, referring mainly to the production of works of art, often presumed to be literary texts in general or at least some literary texts. This could be related to the principles of Kantean aesthetics, but the big names are mostly kept out of the fray.

Vermeer himself answers this criticism by pointing out that his definition of 'action' contains the defining feature of intentionality (1989b:177ff, see chapter 2 above). Behaviour that does not show any intentionality or purpose is thus not regarded as an action (although Vermeer admits there may be other definitions of action). Vermeer places particular emphasis on his view that actions do not *have* a purpose anyway, but that they *are interpreted as* being purposeful by the participants or any observer. In order to be interpreted as purposeful, a particular action must be the result of a free decision for (or against) one of two or more possible modes of acting, including the possibility of not acting at all.

Applying this general principle to translation theory, the idea of purpose can refer to the translational action as a whole, to the target text as result of this action, and to a particular translation unit plus the translation strategy chosen for its transfer (see chapter 3 above and Vermeer 1989a:100ff).

Criticism 2: Not all translations have a purpose.

The second criticism is a particular variant of the first. It maintains that not every translation can be interpreted as purposeful. Since it is also usually brought forward with reference to literature, the general considerations of the previous paragraphs may be applied here as well. There are, however, three specific positions that deserve further attention (cf. Vermeer 1989b:179): (a) the claim that the translator does not have any *specific* purpose in mind when translating 'what is in the source text'; (b) the claim that a specific translation purpose would limit or at least restrict the range of possible translation procedures and thus the range of possible interpretations of the target text in comparison to those of the source text (cf. Newmark 1990:106); and (c) the claim that the translator has no *specific* addressees in mind when translating the source text. These three claims may be answered as follows:

(a) Rendering 'what is *in* the source text' (whatever that may be) would be one possible purpose a translator can opt for on certain grounds; rendering what is '*behind* the source text', the sender's intention, would be another. If there are two possible modes of behaviour (and there are many more!) the translator's choice must be guided by some sort of intention or purpose. Although it may be true that, in the process of translation, "the translator is often compelled to switch somewhere between strict correspondence and compensation; between rule through principle to play [sic]" (Newmark 1990: 106), my own experience as a translator and translation critic has shown me that these procedures are usually not chosen arbitrarily but, in the most successful cases, following a consistent global strategy which, in turn, is guided by the overall purpose the translation is intended to fulfil. Without such a consistent global strategy (which may also consist in avoiding the impression of consistency, if this is the intention!) the target audience will not find any coherence in the translated text, as is shown by some of the examples given in chapter 5 above.

(b) A given translation purpose may of course rule out certain interpretations of a given source text because they are considered pointless for the particular target audience. Examples might include intertextual allusions to source-culture literature or a metalinguistic wordplay on the homophony of two source-language words for an audience which does not know the source language. Yet *one* translation purpose may be precisely to produce exactly the same range of possible interpretations as that offered by the source text. How far this is actually possible is not the point here.

(c) Although in many cases a text producer (hence, also a translator) may not be thinking of a specific addressee or set of addressees, they will often have a vague or fuzzy notion of whom they are addressing or at least a rather clear notion of whom they are *not* addressing. But as soon as text producers try to express themselves in a comprehensible way, they must consciously or unconsciously orient their writing toward some prototypical audience whose possibilities of comprehension can somehow be envisaged.

When Newmark (1990:106) claims that Thomas Mann's *The Magic Mountain* "is addressed not just to intellectuals, but to any seeker after entertainment, knowledge and moral truth" (and, I would add, anyone capable of understanding and appreciating the author's style), he actually defines a possible audience. And when he continues, "...but the translator cannot compromise the technical and biological language of the chapter *Forschungen* for the sake of any targeted readership", I would agree wholeheartedly, since the purpose of that chapter is possibly not to entertain nor to provide knowledge or moral truth, and anyway, purpose-orientation does not generally mean adaptation to target-situation standards. However, the translator must make a decision as soon as there are two or more possible solutions to a translation problem and they differ with regard to receiver-dependent qualities such as acceptability or comprehensibility. For example, in medical terminology in German we have a Latinism *and* a common German term for the same disease (such as *Appendizitis* and *Blinddarmentzündung*), and a choice must be made. As in the case of purpose-relevant features, it might make sense to follow a consistent strategy with regard to receiver orientation as well.

Criticism 3: Functional approaches transgress the limits of translation proper.

Starting from the view that equivalence is a *constitutive* feature of translation, Werner Koller (1995:196) defines translation as

> the result of a text-processing activity, by means of which a source-language text is transposed into a target-language text. Between the resultant text in L2 (the target-language text) and the source text in L1 (the source-language text) there exists a relationship, which can be designated as a translational, or equivalence relationship.

In contrast to earlier definitions of equivalence (see Oettinger's or Catford's in chapter 1 above) Koller here regards equivalence as a rather flexible and relative concept. He sees the equivalence relationship as being defined by a "*double linkage*: firstly by its link to the *source text* and secondly by its link to the *communicative conditions* on the *receiver's* side" (1995:197, emphasis in the original). However, according to Koller, this linkage is no more than a "special relationship" that has to be specified for application in the translation process, the specification being subject to the "*extralinguistic circumstances* conveyed by the [source?] text", the "*connotations* ... conveyed by the [source?] text via *the mode of verbalisation*", the "*text and language norms* (usage norms) which apply to parallel texts in the target language", the "way the [target?] *receiver* is taken into account (*Empfängerbezug*)", and the "*aesthetic* properties of the source-language text" (1995:197, emphasis in the original). Apart from the ambiguities indicated by our insertions in square brackets, these conditions are partly contradictory in that, as Koller himself admits, they cannot all be met at the same time or to the same degree in the one particular translation task. For instance, the text and language norms that apply to parallel texts in the target language may contradict the aesthetic properties of the source-language text. Koller (1989:104) therefore establishes a hierarchy of "equivalence requirements" in order distinguish between, on the one hand, translational text *re*production and "equivalence-guided text production" (such as an expansion explaining a source-culture reality to the target audience) and, on the other, "translation with elements of text revision", which he considers a borderline case, and strictly non-translational revision with translated elements (Koller 1995).

Koller then criticizes *Skopostheorie* for having made the "contours of translation, as the object of study ... steadily vaguer and more difficult to survey" (1995:193). He cites Ammann, a close collaborator of Vermeer's at Heidelberg University, who rejects a terminological differentiation between 'translation proper' and other forms of translational action such as paraphrase or adaptation. What Ammann actually says is as follows:

> On the basis of modern translation theory we can talk of 'translation'
> when a source text (of oral or written nature) has, for a particular
> purpose, been used as a model for the production of a text in the target
> culture. As translator I am also in a position to judge when a source
> text is unsuitable as model for a target culture text, and to propose to
> the client the production of a new text for that target culture. (1989:107-
> 108, trans. Peter Cripps, cited from Koller 1995:194)

Note that Ammann does not actually call 'the production of a new text' a
translation in this context. Yet it is certainly something that translators can
do; it is legitimate translational action since, as we have seen in the conceptual system outlined in chapter 2 above, translational action includes
cross-cultural consulting and cross-cultural technical writing even *without
a source text*.

When the concept of equivalence is relativized as much as it is in Koller's
'linguistic-textual' theory, the main difference between this approach and
functionalism no longer resides in the degree to which adaptive or text-
producing activities are accepted as a process named translation. It seems to
me that we have to look in the opposite direction to find the crucial difference:
Would such a concept of equivalence also apply to the literal translation of
a school certificate (plus explanatory comment) or a side-by-side translation
of a contract for sale, or a word-for-word translation produced for linguistic
purposes, where the target text is precisely *not* expected to conform to any
one of Koller's equivalence frameworks? Pym (1992:212) mentions an example of which I have had personal experience: Spanish sworn translations
(*traducciones juradas*) of legal documents are sometimes "literalist to the
point of illegibility", resulting from a procedure that is traditionally required
in the government exam for sworn translators. Would that satisfy Koller's
apparently open notion of equivalence?

Even though translation scholars and practitioners have already recom-
mended a change of conventions in the particular case of Spanish sworn
translations, I fail to see why a theory should exclude such forms of translational action (*with* source text). After all, the extremely literalist Spanish
versions are called translations and are in fact expected of the translator
(who else would be the person to do this sort of job?). As long as they occur
in professional practice, they should surely be addressed in the realm of
translation studies. The risk, as Dirk Delabastita puts it, is that "a narrow,
normative definition of translation is in danger of being applicable to only a
very few, well-selected cases, and of being unsuitable for a description of
most actual facts" (1989:214).

The functional approach offers the possibility of using one and the same theoretical model to account for both documentary and instrumental forms of translation, including, of course, any form of equivalent translation, whatever the specification of equivalence may be.

Criticism 4: Skopostheorie is not an original theory.

Thanks perhaps to its very generality, the functional approach has been seen by some critics as rather banal. Since functionalism is based on something as obvious as the fact that human actions are guided by their purposes, it cannot claim to be an original theory. As Peter Newmark harshly puts it,

> it is merely common sense that in order to do anything well, you have to know why you are doing it, and that if you're translating a soap advert, you won't do it in the same way as you translate a hymn. The Prague School applied Bühler's functional theory of language to translation many years ago, as did Hartmann and Vernay in their *Sprachwissenschaft und Übersetzen* (1970), but to blow this up into a theory of translatorial action, where the aim becomes a skopos, the translation a translatum, the occasion a commission, the reader a consumer, the translator a professional expert, to point out what Neubert pointed out in the '60s, that translations may be made for various purposes, hardly constitutes an original theory of translation.... (1990:106)

Now, the fact that people have observed apples falling off trees since the happy times of Paradise does not deprive Newton's law of gravity of its originality or, at least, of its importance for modern science. Nor does Newmark's wholesale reproach of plagiarism really hold water on the level of detailed references. In the volume *Sprachwissenschaft und Übersetzen* edited by Hartmann and Vernay in 1970, for example, neither Hartmann nor Vernay apply Bühler's language functions to translation. It is Friedrich Irmen who, in the same volume, refers to Bühler's concepts as constraints on *intralingual* synonymy (on the word level), emphasizing the view that, as such, "they are IRRELEVANT FOR TRANSLATION" (1970:149, emphasis in the original). On the other hand, Neubert's 1968 article about the pragmatic aspects of translation does indeed refer to two purpose-dependent translation types. In the first type, called 'pragmatically equivalent' translation, the pragmatic relations of the source-language text are replaced or, rather, reconstructed by target-language relations, whereas the second type, called 'non-equivalent' translation, reproduces the pragmatic relations of the source text in the target language. This is certainly a very interesting way of coping with the eternal dilemma between source-oriented and target-oriented trans-

114

lation, but it can hardly be called an elaborate theory of translation.

Where Newmark does score a goal is with regard to *Skopos* terminology, particularly in reference to Justa Holz-Mänttäri's works, since it must be admitted that the terms have not helped to further the theory's popularity. The penchant for terminology can partly be explained by German scholarly traditions, where new concepts seem to require new terms. The terminology should also be seen in the light of the particular features of translation studies in German universities, where key positions are still held mainly by philologists or linguists whose main interests are not in the practical aspects of the translation profession nor even in translation teaching. In this situation, Holz-Mänttäri and Vermeer, who have been practitioners and teachers themselves, sought to emphasize the practice-oriented nature of their approach by choosing terms related to economic or industrial settings. In the present book, I have simplified and anglicized the terminology as far as was possible, hopefully without betraying the authors' theoretical or methodological intentions.

Although I have been brought up with the German terminology myself, I admit I am not always happy with the result. One of the reasons is that the terms sometimes lead to misunderstandings, no matter how much they might be receiver-oriented. To take just one example, when talking about material text transfer, Anthony Pym questions the location of the 'translation purpose':

> ...if the translational product's purpose and constitutive elements are seen as residing in the target culture before the translation is actually carried out, surely there is nothing of significance to be transferred anyway, since everything of importance is always already there? Is not transfer then entirely illusory? (Pym 1996:338)

If I understand him right, Vermeer's view is that the *Skopos* (a static concept) is indeed located in the target culture, defining the situation in which the target text is going to be received. On the other hand, the *purpose* (a dynamic concept) has its origin in the source situation; it is the 'drive' directing the object to be transferred toward its aim. In most contexts, this nuance is not of vital importance, which may account for Vermeer's using the terms as synonyms.

As for purposefulness being an empty or meaningless concept in translation theory, I believe it is not purposefulness *as such* that helps us gain a better understanding of what translation is about but the *plurality* of purposes. Comparing translations of various texts in various situations at various moments in history we find that different purposes can very often explain why translators have chosen different techniques or procedures to solve similar or analogous problems. And if we look a little more closely at the variables determining the purpose or *Skopos* (addressees, temporal and spatial conditions, initiators' intentions, and so on) we might even be able to establish a correlation between some of these variables and the solutions chosen by translators. Such research, however, still remains to be done on a large scale.

Criticism 5: Functionalism is not based on empirical findings.

This leads us to another criticism which has been brought forward, most notably by Werner Koller: it is claimed that functional models of translation have a theoretical-speculative approach rather than an empirical one (cf. also Lörscher 1988:80f, similarly Pym 1996:338). Referring to several apodictic statements presented by Reiss and Vermeer (for example, "Translators offer just so much information and in just the manner which they consider optimal for the target-text recipient in view of their translation", Reiss and Vermeer 1984:123), Koller asks the following questions:

> Do these sentences refer to a given set of translations, say in German, i.e. are they based on empirical investigations which justify results of the type: The analysis of 1000 translations from English into German reveals that in 95% of cases the important factor for the translation/ interpretation was the respective translator's decision as to what and how to translate/interpret? Or is the idea that: For a translator/interpreter to translate well, s/he must decide what and how to translate? (1995:215, note 21)

Koller is quite justified in asking this kind of question. To my knowledge, the principles of *Skopostheorie* have so far not been based on any thorough analysis of large, possibly electronically-held corpora. They are founded on observations of translation practice in various fields, as indeed would seem to be Koller's own remarks about equivalence being a constitutive feature of translation and the five equivalence frameworks he suggests to explain certain features of some texts and their translations.

This is not the place for a contest in empiricism. Both approaches will have to make use of corpus-based empirical studies to verify or falsify their working hypotheses. Since the functional model was born in translator-training institutions, its occasional normative aspects are not just accidental. The focus on differences rather than on similarities between source-text and target-text functions could also be due to a strong orientation toward professional practice in business and international settings. The segment of translational practice you are looking at certainly influences what you find: when considering literary examples, Koller may well notice some striving after equivalence (in a *very* relative sense); when surveying a wider professional context, others are more likely to see adaptations to target-culture norms, conventions or pragmatics as typical features required by customers. As a matter of fact, industrial translators or interpreters, who might be considered representatives of a certain 'empirical' awareness, often emphasize the broad range of tasks that they are called on to carry out (cf. Stellbrink 1987, Ammann 1989b, Manuel Vermeer 1989, Schmitt 1989).

Criticism 6: Functionalism produces mercenary experts.

Thanks to this last aspect, many practising translators find that functional-ist models give them more responsibility and self-confidence in a society where translating is still mainly considered a 'serving profession'. And as Kussmaul puts it, "serving does not usually go together with a well devel-oped ego" (1995:32). How does this fit in with the fact that quite a few critics reproach functionalism for producing "mercenary experts, able to fight under the flag of any purpose able to pay them" (Pym 1996:338)?

This criticism is due to the idea that the translation purpose is defined by the translation brief, which is part of the translation commission given by the initiator, who is thus regarded as the person who 'tells the translator how to translate'. There are two misunderstandings underlying this view.

First, we have to distinguish between the translation *Skopos* (in the sense of 'aim'), which requires certain qualities of the target text, and the actual procedures the translator uses to achieve this aim. The *Skopos* is indeed determined by the initiator's needs and wishes *with regard to the communi-cative action* they intend to realize by means of the target text, whereas the actual procedures are entirely up to the translator as a competent expert in translation. Clients sometimes boast of sufficient knowledge of the target language (if they only had the time, they would do the translation work themselves, but they have so many more important things to do...); they may even try to tell the translator how to translate. Worse, they often think of translation as a simple code-switching operation, based on their own expe-rience in foreign-language classes or on dubious advertisements for machine-translation systems that 'translate' much faster and more effec-tively than any human translator. There is no reason why professional translators should imitate the often limited competence of their clients.

Second, functionalist theories do not tell the translator how to translate, no more than should clients. Criticizing functionalist 'dogmatism', Newmark (1990:105) states that translation

> is a fractured subject which is peculiarly unsuitable for a single
> integrated theory, a dogma, a blanket statement that will embrace any
> type of text. In a process and a practice where one often has to think of

so many things at the same time,... where rule or principle is occasionally set aside for the instinctual pleasure of sheer play, no one thought-through (*durchdachte*) theory is ever going to cover every translation problem.

The task of a general theory is not to instruct practitioners about how to do their jobs (this opinion is shared by Koller 1995:200). Theories may help practitioners observe and reflect on what they are doing, on the consequences that one or another decision may have for the communicative effect of the target text they are producing. According to Holmes (1988:98), this in itself is a justification for translation theory:

> If translation theory, even at its present state, can give us some more awareness of what we are doing as translators and help us to think and become conscious of our activity, then I think it has fulfilled an important role.

Moreover, if translators do not just follow the 'instinctual pleasure of sheer play', they should be able to justify their translations by rational arguments. This ability gives them not only self-awareness but also self-confidence, and self-confidence enables them to become equal partners in their negotiations with clients.

One of the main ideas of functionalist approaches, most notably in Justa Holz-Mänttäri's work, is to give the translator the prestige of being an 'expert in intercultural communication' (the change in terminology is strategic in this case) and thus a responsible partner for clients. In this sense one might also talk about 'client education'. If translators succeed in gaining their clients' confidence, then their responsible decisions will be more readily accepted. This can happen even when the target text does not reveal the nature of its relationship with the source text to the eyes of a non-expert in translation at first sight. Vermeer also points out the importance of cooperation:

> Collaborating in the communicative act in such a way as to enable the achievement of the *Skopos* is the main and foremost task of translators. We may well call it their social task, for they are the experts who know how to socially bring about transcultural communication and lead it to its intended aim. (Vermeer 1990b, ms., cited in Witte 1992:122)

In my opinion, translators are treated much more like 'mercenaries' or 'servants' when they are asked to subordinate their own judgement of what has to be done and why it has to be done in favour of the structural features of a text that was produced in another culture for different addressees and some-times also for different purposes. Such prescriptiveness, which is not at all that of functionalist approaches, does not even allow translators to negoti-ate with their apparent master, the mythical source text.

Pym also asks if functionalist theories generate "a way of discerning between good and bad purposes" (1996:338). To answer this, I note that I have introduced the notion of loyalty into functionalism, precisely as an ethical principle (1988 and chapter 9 below). However, to discern between "good and bad translation strategies" (Pym ibid.) is not a problem of ethics but of translational competence: good strategies are those most able to carry out the desired purpose.

Criticism 7: Functionalism does not respect the original.

Functionalist approaches are often criticized for changing or even betraying originals. This criticism is closely linked to the previous one, since it is based on the assumption that when translators take into account the needs and expectations of their target audience they must necessarily lose sight of 'the' source text.

To answer this criticism, I should point out that functionalist approaches are based on a sociological concept of what a text is. The form in which the source text lies before the translator is a product of the many variables of the situation (time, place, addressees) in which it originated, and the way this form is interpreted and understood by the translator or any other re-ceiver is guided by the variables of the new reception situation, including, of course, the translator's competence in text analysis, which may help them to relativize their own standpoint.

While the broader textual-linguistic equivalence approach developed by Koller and others stretches the idea of a translation's 'double linkage' to both the source and target sides so far as to almost blur the borderline between translations and non-translations, narrower linguistic approaches still start from the autonomy or authority of a source text that must not be touched in the translation process. Newmark, for example, deplores the "oversimplification" inherent in functionalism, lamenting "the concentration on the message at the sacrifice of the richness of the meaning and to the detriment of the authority of the source-language text" (1990: 106). The problem, however, is that anyone judging "the richness of the meaning" and "the authority of the source language text" has to do so from their own point of view in time and space. No one can claim to have *the* source text at their disposal to transform it into *the* target text.

This criticism is probably due to Vermeer's claim to have 'dethroned' the source text. But dethroning does not imply murder or dumping; it simply means that the source text, or more precisely, its linguistic and stylistic features, is no longer regarded as the one and only yardstick for a translation. After all, the concept of the original text simply cannot be maintained uncritically after all we have learnt about text reception in the last few decades.

Criticism 8: Functionalism is a theory of adaptation.

Closely linked with the previous criticism, functionalism is sometimes seen as no more than a theory of adaptation. If the source text is no longer regarded as the only yardstick, the other pole – the participants and conditions of the target situation – must naturally come more into focus. In order to emphasize this change of perspective, functionalists have probably insisted more on cases where adaptive procedures ensure the functionality of the original than on all the other cases where documentary translation forms are called for. This may have produced the impression that functionalist models in general, or *Skopostheorie* in particular, are mainly models of adaptation. Yet this impression is really no more than a form of 'selective reception', a quite normal process whereby, confronted by a large offer of information, we pay attention to only those items that succeed in awaking our interest or our disapproval. As has been shown in chapter 4 above, the functional approach accounts for all sorts of both documentary and instrumental modes of translation.

Criticism 9: Functionalism does not work in literary translation.

Literary translators or literary scholars interested in translation often see functionalism as something that is simply not meant for them. The presuppositions underlying this view are related to criticisms 1 and 2 above (in that they challenge the purposefulness of literary texts and their translations), to criticism 3 (they assume a narrower concept of translation proper) and criticism 7 (they emphasize the authoritative status of the source text in literary translation).

These critics normally accept that functionalism works for operating instructions, news texts, advertisements and the like, texts whose language is clearly instrumental. In these cases the critics welcome adaptive procedures and even substitutions, paraphrases, omissions, expansions, indeed any change that adds to the comprehensibility or acceptability of the target text. In literary translation, however, the source text has a different status. This is probably what Newmark is hinting at when he writes, "The more important the language of a text, the more closely it should be translated, and its cultural component transferred' (1990:105). Or again, says Newmark,

> Far from dethroning the source language text, rejecting it, deverbalizing it, vaporizing it, transforming it, ignoring it, I look hard at it. If it is good, I want to render it accurately through translation; if it is defective, I want to expose it through translation. (1990:105)

In his article 'The Literary Translator between Original and Market Demands', Rainer Kohlmayer (1988:149ff) analyzes several examples taken from the works of functionalist scholars: a fragment from James Joyce's *Ulysses* discussed by Hönig and Kussmaul (1982:110-117); Georges Pompidou's speech on the occasion of De Gaulle's death analyzed by Reiss and Vermeer (1984:215f), a speech by Cicero discussed by Vermeer (1979:6f) and a reference to Homer's *Iliad* made by Reiss and Vermeer (1984:104). Kohlmayer's resulting criticism with regard to the applicability of *Skopostheorie* to literary translation is based on some of the arguments that have been dealt with in the previous paragraphs: Apart from so-called 'light fiction', which has much in common with pragmatic texts for practical use, literary texts cannot be regarded as purposeful (see criticism 1); if their translation is guided by target purposes, they are reduced to consumer-oriented 'light fiction' (see criticism 2a); purpose-orientation in translation tends to limit the possibilities of grasping the entire meaning potential of the original from the start (see criticism 2b); there is no way of knowing who the target audience is and what its needs and expectations are (see criticism 2c); the normative orientation toward this assumed audience enforces linguistic and cultural stereotypes, limiting the originality and transformative power of translated literature and infringing on the authoritative status of the source text (see criticism 7); a functional translator is thus a traitor to the source text (see criticism 5).

Interestingly enough, some defence of source-text 'dethronement' comes from what is known as Descriptive Translation Studies. Theo Hermans, for example, maintains that

> Taking the supremacy of the original for granted from the start, the study of translation then serves merely to demonstrate that original's outstanding qualities by highlighting the errors and inadequacies of any number of translations of it. The outcome, needless to say, is an invariably source-oriented exercise, which, by constantly holding the original up as an absolute standard and touchstone, becomes repetitive, predictable and prescriptive - the implicit norm being a transcendental and utopian conception of translation as reproducing the original, the whole original and nothing but the original (1985:8f).

In chapter 5 I have tried to present some provocative functionalist ideas on literary translation. The examples presented there hopefully show that a considerable number of problems in literary translation can be approached from a functionalist standpoint without jeopardizing the 'originality' of the source text. To make the originality of the source show through in the target text is, of course, a possible translation purpose. The problem is whether this can be done by simply reproducing what is *in* the text, since what is original in one culture may be less so in another, and vice versa. The concept of function-plus-loyalty (see chapter 8) could perhaps make the functionalist approach even more directly applicable in literary translation.

Criticism 10: Functionalism is marked by cultural relativism.

Anthony Pym has described functionalism as being marked by cultural relativism (cf. 1992b, 1993b, 1996). I would in principle agree with this statement, but I do not take it as a negative criticism. The emphasis on cultural relativism in functional theories has to be seen as a reaction against the universalistic tendencies in earlier theoretical approaches to translation. And it has, of course, pedagogical implications in that it makes students aware of the culture-specificity (in the sense of non-generalizability) of their own patterns of linguistic and non-linguistic behaviour. We should thus speak more exactly of cultural anti-universalism. When Pym observes

> that [in functionalist approaches] emphasis is placed on radically different and mutually distinct cultures rather than on translation between real or virtual neighbors in the process of changing their intercultural relations (1996: 338),

he implies that 'cultures' are confronted as holistic entities or systems. However, as has been pointed out in chapter 2 above, culture-specificity may be observed precisely in the 'rich points' of contact between two cultures or groups, since cultures cannot be conceived as monolithic or concentric systems today (and probably never could). Functionalism does not imply any *a priori* dominance of target-culture forms of behaviour in the way translators cope with cultural conflicts, as Pym seems to assume. Indeed, the anti-universalism of functionalist approaches is meant precisely to avoid one-sided purposes or cultural imperialism, as we shall see at the end of chapter 9.

8. Function plus Loyalty

When I was trained as a translator at the School of Translation and Interpreting at Heidelberg University in the 1960s, translation theory as we know it today had not been invented. Training mainly involved looking over the shoulders of experienced translators and trying to find out, through a perilous process of trial and error, what distinguished a 'good' translation from a 'bad' one. As can be seen from the first publications on translation methodology which appeared in those years (such as Reiss 1971), equivalence was tacitly presupposed to be the guiding principle of the translation process, even though certain teachers, or certain occasions, seemed to demand different yardsticks. In any case, it was usually the source text or some of its features (text typologies had not been invented) that were declared to be responsible for the change in strategy. It was the source text that required faithfulness, even with regard to punctuation in some literary or legal translations, and it was the source text, too, that demanded adaptation of some examples or culture-bound concepts to target-culture conventions or expectations in other translations such as newspaper texts.

In this situation *Skopostheorie* fell on fertile ground. Not only did it account for different strategies in different translation situations, in which source texts are not the only factor involved, but it also coincided with a change of paradigm in quite a few disciplines, among them linguistics, which had developed a stronger focus on communication as a social, culture-bound occurrence, on the individuals involved, on the spatiotemporal conditions of communication, and on communicative intentions and functions. *Skopostheorie* seemed to be exactly the translational model that was needed. It was

- *pragmatic*, accounting for the situational conditions of communicative interaction and, accordingly, for the needs and expectations of the addressees or prospective receivers of the target text and even making the target receiver the most important yardstick of translational decisions;
- *culture-oriented*, giving consideration to the culture-specific forms of verbal and nonverbal behaviour involved in translation;
- *consistent*, able to establish a coherent theoretical and methodological framework that could serve as a guideline for an intersubjective justification of the translator's decisions in any type or form of translation task, permitting any translation procedures that would lead to a functional target text;
- *practical*, accounting for all the forms of transcultural communication needed in professional translation practice;

- *normative*, in the sense of giving the translator a guideline as to the best or safest ways to attain a particular translation purpose;
- *comprehensive*, because target function was considered to be the main standard for any translation process, one possible function being the presentation of a target text whose communicative effects were equivalent to those of the source text; and
- *expert*, in the sense that it attributed to the translator the prestige of being an expert in their field, competent to make purpose-adequate decisions with full responsibility with regard to their partners.

In short, this model seemed just too good to be true. So where was the flaw?

My personal point of view has partly been shaped through the influence of my teachers, among them Katharina Reiss. Yet I see two interdependent limitations to the *Skopos* model as it has been presented here. One concerns the culture-specificity of translational models; the other has to do with the relationship between the translator and the source-text author.

Like the concept of equivalence, *Skopostheorie* claims to be a general or universal model of translation (see the title of Reiss and Vermeer 1984). Although Vermeer allows for a relationship of 'intertextual coherence' or fidelity to hold between the source and target texts, the demand for fidelity is subordinate to the *Skopos* rule. As we have seen, the main idea of *Skopostheorie* could be paraphrased as 'the translation purpose justifies the translation procedures'. Now, this seems acceptable whenever the translation purpose is in line with the communicative intentions of the original author. But what happens if the translation brief requires a translation whose communicative aims are contrary to or incompatible with the author's opinion or intention? In this case, the *Skopos* rule could easily be interpreted as 'the end justifies the means', and there would be no restriction to the range of possible ends.

In a general theory, this might be acceptable enough, since one could always argue that general theories do not have to be directly applicable. Yet translator training, like translation itself, does not take place in general or 'deculturalized' surroundings. Students are trained to be translators within one particular culture community (or perhaps two culture communities) at a given point in history. Any application of the general theory to translator training must thus take these particular settings into consideration.

Looking at the history of translation and translations, we find that at different times and in different parts of the world people have had different concepts of what a good translation is or should be. These notions sometimes vary according to the text type in question or depend on the self-esteem of the receiving culture with regard to the source culture (cf. Bassnet-McGuire

1991:39ff). According to the prevailing concept of translation, readers might expect, for example, that the target text gives exactly the author's opinion; other cultures might want it to be a faithful reproduction of the formal source-text features; still others could praise archaizing translations or ones that are not at all faithful reproductions but a comprehensible readable texts. Translators must take these expectations into account. This does not mean that translators are always obliged to do exactly what the readers expect. Yet there is a moral responsibility not to deceive them (cf. Nord 1991:94f). Of course, it may be difficult to know exactly what readers expect of a translation, since this is a field where extensive empirical research remains to be done. For the time being, though, translators must rely on conjectures and on the scarce feedback they get from their clients and readers.

Let me call 'loyalty' this responsibility translators have toward their partners in translational interaction. Loyalty commits the translator bilaterally to the source and the target sides. It must not be mixed up with fidelity or faithfulness, concepts that usually refer to a relationship holding between the source and the target *texts*. Loyalty is an interpersonal category referring to a social relationship between *people*.

In the general model, loyalty would be an empty slot that, in a particular translation task, is filled by the demands of the specific translation concepts of the cultures in question. For example, if the target culture expects a translation to be a literal reproduction of the original, translators cannot simply translate in a non-literal way without telling the target audience what they have done and why. It is the translator's task to mediate between the two cultures, and mediation cannot mean imposing one's culture-specific concept on members of another culture community.

In introducing the loyalty principle into the functionalist model, I would also hope to solve the second problem I see in radical functionalism. This concerns the relationship between the source-text author and the translator. Normally, since authors are rarely experts in translation, they are likely to insist on a faithful rendering of the source text's surface structures. Only if they trust the translator's loyalty will they consent to any changes or adaptations needed to make the translation work in the target culture. And this confidence would again strengthen the translator's social prestige as a responsible and trustworthy partner.

In this context, loyalty means that the target-text purpose should be compatible with the original author's intentions. This may not be a problem where the sender's intentions are evident from the communicative situation in which the source text is or was used, as with operating instructions or commercial advertisements. In these cases we may speak of 'conventional' intentions linked with certain text types. In other cases, the analysis of extratextual factors such as author, time, place, or medium may shed some light on what may have been the sender's intentions (cf. Nord [1988] 1991:47ff). However, it can be difficult to elicit the sender's intentions in cases where we don't have enough information about the original situation (as is the case with ancient texts) or where the source-text situation is so different from the target-text situation that there is no way of establishing a direct link between the source-text author and the target-text readers. In these cases, a documentary translation may be the only way to solve the dilemma. Sometimes a thorough analysis of intratextual function markers helps the translator to find out about the communicative intentions that may have guided the author.

The loyalty principle thus adds two important qualities to the functional approach. Since it obliges the translator to take account of the difference between culture-specific concepts of translation prevailing in the two cultures involved in the translation process, it turns *Skopostheorie* into an *anti-universalist* model, and since it induces the translator to respect the sender's individual communicative intentions, as far as they can be elicited, it reduces the prescriptiveness of 'radical' functionalism.

My personal version of the functionalist approach thus stands on two pillars: function *plus* loyalty (see Nord [1988] 1991:28ff and 1993:17ff). It is precisely the combination of the two principles that matters, even though there may be cases where they seem to contradict each other. Function refers to the factors that make a target text work in the intended way in the target situation. Loyalty refers to the interpersonal relationship between the translator, the source-text sender, the target-text addressees and the initiator. Loyalty limits the range of justifiable target-text functions for one particular source text and raises the need for a negotiation of the translation assignment between translators and their clients.

Let's see what this means in practice:

Example: In his book *En Cuba*, written after a first visit to Cuba following the Revolution in 1959, the Nicaraguan priest Ernesto Cardenal presents a subjective, politically biased view of Cuban society. He is enthusiastic about the changes brought about by Fidel Castro's government. At no moment does he pretend to be objective, and the reader cannot fail to be impressed, even though they may not share Cardenal's views. The German translation published in 1972 (*In Kuba. Bericht einer Reise*) nevertheless gives the impression of a moderate, rather objective report of the author's journey, with the reader constantly being reminded that all that glitters is not gold. The German reader is most likely to believe the author has adopted a critical attitude toward Castro's regime, without realizing that this conclusion is not in line with the author's intention. The German readers expect that a translation published under the original author's name will present the original author's opinion. At the same time, the author probably expects the translation to reproduce his personal viewpoints. Both the author and the target audience are deceived, although the translation may have been quite functional from the publisher's standpoint, who in the early 1970s may not have dared to confront German readers with a 'pro-Communist' author. The translator should have argued this point with the initiator or perhaps have refused to produce the translation on ethical grounds.

Within the framework of the function-plus-loyalty approach, an instrumental translation can be chosen only in those cases where the sender's intention is not directed exclusively at source-culture receivers but can also be transferred to a target-culture audience. This would have been possible with Ernesto Cardenal's book if the initiator had not given priority to commercial considerations. When this is not the case, the translation should probably be carried out in documental function, informing the reader about the source-text situation, perhaps in a few introductory lines, and thus giving the target addressees an indication that they are reading a translated text.

On the other hand, loyalty may require the adaptation of certain translation units even when the author wishes to maintain them unchanged. This can be seen in the following case:

Example: In a textbook on the philosophy of education, the Spanish author harshly describes someone else's standpoint as being *"para vomitar"* ("it makes one vomit"). The German translator decided not to ask the author for permission to adapt this expression to the conventions of German textbooks; she simply translated the phrase by the German equivalent of "almost unbearable", which was the nearest she could come to emotionality without risking the author's credibility as a serious scholar. If she had asked him, he would probably have insisted on a literal translation, as he had done on other occasions. In his own language and culture, the author himself is responsible for the effect he creates, and his reputation perhaps gives him a kind of fool's licence in his own country. In the target culture, though, it was the translator's responsibility to make sure the book was appropriately received; in this situation she had to take target-culture expectations into account.

The function-plus-loyalty model is also an answer to those critics who argue that the functional approach leaves translators free to do whatever they like with any source text, or worse, what their clients like. The loyalty principle takes account of the legitimate interests of the three parties involved: initiators (who want a particular type of translation), target receivers (who expect a particular relationship between original and target texts) and original authors (who have a right to demand respect for their individual intentions and expect a particular kind of relationship between their text and its translation). If there is any conflict between the interests of the three partners of the translator, it is the translator who has to mediate and, where necessary, seek the understanding of all sides.

9. Future Perspectives

Functionalism is widely seen as appealing to common sense. One might thus assume that once 'discovered' (not as something unheard of before, but as something that had always been there without anyone really noticing) it would spread like wildfire through the world of translation studies. Yet this is not quite what is happening.

Of course, functional translation has always been widely practised in professional contexts, at least in those parts with which I have come into contact (so much for cultural relativism!), where clients usually insist on smooth, conventional target texts that do not betray their translational origin to the unbiased reader's eyes. Nor am I alone in this opinion; the following quotations may stand for many others:

> 'Cultural' text adaptation: The problem is often neglected, but there are striking exceptions, such as the Scandinavian electronics company that found it worthwhile to produce three versions of their French promotion: one for France, one for Switzerland and one for Canada. The Belgians, presumably, had to muddle through with the version intended for France. (Berglund 1987:11)

> The purpose of the majority of translations produced today is to function as independent, 'autonomous' or 'self-sufficient' texts. Typically, e.g. in tourist information, directions for use, and manuals, an institution or a company or corporation takes the place of author and translator. The text contains no explicit indication who actually authored and/or translated it, or whether the text is a translation or not. Obviously, therefore, whenever texts are produced through translation, no trace of this must be detectable in the body of the text either. (Jakobsen 1994a:58)

In the academic world, however, the situation is rather difficult to grasp. In what follows, I will nevertheless try to give a brief geographical survey, describing who is working where and outlining some of the main fields of current functionalist research. In order to allow the scholars to speak for themselves, I will quote a paragraph or so from their works. For the benefit of the audience of this book (*Skopos*!) I will focus on quotations in English, in order to (purpose!) provide incentives for further reading.

In the German-speaking area, the representatives of the first generation of functionalism (Reiss, Vermeer, Holz-Mänttäri) retired some time ago, and the second generation has generally entered the training of university students (such as Hönig, Kussmaul, Kupsch-Losereit, Schmitt, myself and others whose writings have been mentioned already). Other members of this second generation have gone further afield: Heidrun Witte, a close collaborator and disciple of Vermeer at Heidelberg University, has been teaching in Spain for a number of years; Margaret Ammann, also a collaborator of Vermeer's, has entered industrial translation practice. She is a Portuguese-German bilingual and practising translator and interpreter, whose publications focus mainly on translator training and curriculum development (cf. Ammann 1989c, Ammann and Vermeer 1990).

A representative of the still very scarce third generation in Germany is Susanne Göpferich, whose doctoral dissertation on the implications of an LSP (language for special purposes) text typology for the translation of technical and scientific texts (Göpferich 1995a, 1995b) will certainly become a standard work in the field. Her analysis of English and German technical and scientific text types has produced, among much else, the following interesting findings:

> Juridical-normative texts, for example, contain the most rigid syntactic standard phrases; the frequency of such phrases in this text type is relatively high. For translation didactics this means that juridical-normative texts could be used when students are being taught how to treat syntactic standard phrases in translation. What is most important in this respect is that since syntactic standard phrases are often culture-specific, they cannot be transferred into the target language without content adaptations if they are to serve the same communicative functions. Thus, for example, British patent specifications always begin with the standard phrase: *We, ..., do hereby declare the invention for which we pray that a patent may be granted to us, and the method by which it is to be performed, to be particularly described in and by the following statement:* .... This phrase has no syntactic equivalent in German patent specifications, where only the name of the patent applicant (given in the British standard phrase) appears on the title page in a kind of list and must be rendered accordingly (provided the target text is to fulfil the same communicative function as the source text). (Göpferich 1995b:321)

There is a small nucleus of second-generation functionalists around Mary Snell-Hornby's Chair of Translation Studies at Vienna University, among them Franz Pöchhacker, mentioned in chapter 6, and Klaus Kaindl, whose interesting study on the translation of operas (1995) shows a distinctly interdisciplinary approach. There is also a rather strong group of followers of Holz-Mänttäri in Finland, some of whom are writing in German. These include Hanna Risku, who may already be regarded as belonging to the third generation (cf. Risku 1991), Roland Freihoff (cf. Freihoff 1991) and Jürgen Schopp, who focuses on the relationship between typography, layout and text in translation, a field that is becoming increasingly important with the rise of desktop publishing and other electronic means of text configuration (cf. Schopp 1995). Roland Freihoff compares the translator with an architect: "The translator is an architect who is told to create a building within a framework fixed in cooperation with the client" (1991:43, my translation).

Some other Finnish functionalists are writing in English. This is the case of Riitta Oittinen and Tiina Puurtinen, both researchers in the field of translating for children, or Erkka Vuorinen, a part-time translator for one of the largest daily newspapers in Finland, who is doing research on the cultural aspects of news translation. Riitta Oittinen, a translator and illustrator of children's books herself, draws on Mikhail Bakhtin's notion of dialogue in literary reception (cf. Bakhtin 1990):

> "The text flourishes in a context of authority," says George Steiner (1978:13). So does a translation. But living under the authority of the original leads to translating on the surface, word-for-word, meaning-for-meaning. The assumption is made that denying or relativizing the authority of the original inevitably leads to disrespect for it. This is not the case. On the contrary, a dialogic relationship rather than submission to the authority of the original means placing a high value on the original and finding ways to express the original in a fresh and living way for the reading child. The famous Swedish children's book-lover Lennart Hellsing points out that creating new versions of classics is the only way to keep them alive. He also points out that keeping strictly to the originals means 'murdering' them as art. (Oittinen 1990: 49)

In her doctoral dissertation, Oittinen takes a decidedly functionalist view of translating for children:

> One question clearly takes precedence when we translate for children: For whom? We translate for the benefit of the future readers of the text, children who will read or listen to the stories, children who will interpret the stories in their own ways. This question also brings up the issue of authority. If we simply aim at conveying 'all' of the original message, at finding some positivistic 'truth' in the 'original', we forget the purpose and the function of the whole translation process. However, if we stress the importance of, for instance, the 'readability' of the target-language text (or rather the whole situation), we give priority

to the child as a reader, as someone who understands, as someone who actively participates in the reading event. (1993:4)

Tiina Puurtinen has investigated the linguistic acceptability in translated children's literature in Finland:

> In adult literature, a translation may be acceptable even if it differs considerably from original TL [target-language] texts, but in translated children's literature tolerance for such strangeness is likely to be much lower. It can be inferred from book reviews that Finnish translations of children's books are not expected to show linguistic deviations from originally Finnish books, i.e. both are expected to be governed by similar norms. Conspicuous features of translationese are frowned upon by literary critics and other adult readers as well. (Puurtinen 1995:45)

Erkka Vuorinen is working on a project called 'Crossing Cultural Barriers in International News Transmission'. With regard to the eternal question of source-text status, he points out that

> it is evident that the same status-related factors that govern text processing in general also apply to translation. For example, one factor which plays an important role in translation is the position occupied by the source text in the source culture. Not all source texts have similar positions and existences prior to translation: some have a source-culture existence which is totally independent of translation; some may have been produced with an eye to (possible) translation; some function as pilot texts for translation only and have no existence in the source culture apart from that. (1995:98)

At the Copenhagen Business School in Denmark, Arnt Lykke Jakobsen is also drawing on functional insights in his research on LSP translation and the teaching of translation (Jakobsen 1993, 1994a,b). In his teaching, he is experimenting with the similarities of translation and text production, integrating translating and writing techniques:

> placing translation within the whole spectrum of text production and consistently exposing students to authentic parallel texts will help them develop greater critical awareness of acceptability norms and textual models in the target language, both when they are translating into their native and into a foreign language. Also, by not demanding real translation until quite late in the course, we believe we have mini-

mised the risk that translation tasks result in pseudo-text production. (Jakobsen 1994b:146)

In the Netherlands, one of the centres of translator training is located at Utrecht University, where we also find a young representative of the third generation of functionalists. Jacqueline Hulst recently published her doctoral thesis *Focus on the Target Text* (written in Dutch, with an extensive summary in English), in which she presents a functional model of translation criticism. In this model, 'the main focus is on the target text as an independent entity , whereas the study of the relationship between the target text and original has a secondary position' (Hulst 1995:257). The model is based on a multi-layered concept of 'connectivity', establishing a link between the intended function of the text and the linguistic means used to achieve this function. Translation criticism then consists in comparing the connectivity relations observed in the source text with those found in the target text. According to Hulst, the comparison should allow the critic

> to relate the possible differences between source and target texts with respect to the organization of structure and content to the intended communicative purpose. Some differences may be called 'neutral', that is, they do not affect the realization of the text act and the communicative purpose. When differences do affect the realization of the intended function, they may do so either positively or negatively. Differences with a positive effect might be called 'functionally adequate'...
> (1995:261)

Heidrun Witte, whose main interest is in the cultural aspects of translation and translation teaching (see Witte 1987, Vermeer and Witte 1990, Witte 1992), has been involved in translator training in Las Palmas de Gran Canaria (Spain) for a number of years. Thanks to her and the missionary work of some other adherents of functionalism in various parts of Spain and Latin America, functionalist ideas have become widely known and in part accepted in the Spanish-speaking world. According to Witte,

> It is essential that students are made to understand that bearing in mind the target situation does not in itself entail a specific translation strategy, but first of all it means anticipating the possible effects different translation alternatives may have upon the target receiver. However, our stress on the relevance of culture differences must not lead to a static idea of culture specificity and should therefore be backed up with discussion of the relativity of 'detecting' culture-specific traits.

> Although translators may acquire a relatively high degree of 'biculturality', they will, like everyone else, never be able to loosen themselves completely from their primary culture. To a certain degree, they will therefore always perceive foreign cultures from their own 'culture-bound' perspective. (1994:74)

In the English-speaking world, *Skopostheorie* and functionalist approaches have been gaining ground only very recently, thanks to (still very few) translations of some basic theoretical texts (as in Chesterman 1989) and a growing number of publications in English. Yet the language barrier does not seem to have been overcome. As we have seen, functionalism is inadequately presented in supposedly general texts like Gentzler's *Contemporary Translation Theories* (1993); it could also help moderate the indiscriminate discontent expressed by Hewson and Martin in their so-called *Redefining Translation* (1991), where the only German theory cited is the English version of Wilss's *Science of Translation*.

One of the few English-language scholars defending a functionalist perspective is Roda P. Roberts in Ottawa, who in a 1992 article argues that the literary translator's guide is the function of the translation rather than the functions of language or the source text. Nevertheless, Roberts draws more on Sager's translation types (1983:122f) than on *Skopostheorie* as such, although Reiss and Vermeer's *Grundlegung* is listed in the references. Sager himself, who in a 1993 text adopts a very broad practice-oriented concept of translation (including excerpts, abstracts and gist translations) maintains a critical distance with respect to the main functionalist theories, which he judges on the basis of a 1986 article by Vermeer.

Interestingly enough, functionalist approaches fall on very fertile ground in what from a eurocentric point of view might be called 'exotic' cultures (notably Indonesia, Thailand, India, and Brazil). When I'm in these countries giving seminars on functional approaches, I often find myself virtually preaching to the converted. As a European in Asia, for instance, you are a living example of the dangers of cultural fallacies; students are constantly aware of cultural differences. In Central Europe, on the other hand, many people struggle to believe there are cultural differences between France and Italy, Belgium and the Netherlands, Denmark and Germany. Perhaps the use of international languages in Europe, notably English , adds to the illusion that we are all one harmonious family. Yet the biggest culture shock I ever experienced was when I lived in Austria for a year and a half: speaking the same language does not prevent you from culturally putting your foot in your mouth every second time you open it.

Nevertheless, with the rapid growth in the number of translator-training institutions, functionalist ideas about translation teaching are increasingly accepted in Eastern Europe, in Riga (Latvia), Warsaw (Poland), Ljubljana (Slovenia), Prague (Czech Republic) and Moscow (Russia), to name but a few centres.

The above list of scholars, centres and research projects is not intended to be exhaustive. It is no doubt biased toward the scholars personally known to me or whose work I have read. There are certainly many more people working on projects that will not only elaborate the basic ideas of function-alism but also improve its application to various fields and, above all, develop its importance for the training of competent, responsible professionals.

These perspectives should prove important for the future. As a final example, let me draw your attention to a recent development that shows how functional translation can help change power relations in modern societies.

Functional Translation and Democracy

In South Africa, the ANC's close to two-thirds majority in the first demo-cratic elections was due in no small part to its massive translation effort. All campaign documentation was translated into the nine African languages for the first time. After the political changes brought about by the elections, translation conventions were radically changed by the increasing demand for translations in the fields of administration, finance, insurance, law, health and medicine, often into languages which lacked the corresponding terminologies and means of expression has even led to a radical change in translation conventions. As Walker et al. put it,

> Traditionally, adaptation and reformulation skills did not form part of translation programmes, because they were not compatible with the conventional notion of 'mirror-image' translation based on equiva-lence between source text (ST) and target text (TT). Translation trainers were accustomed to regarding the ST as the yardstick against which translation students should judge their translations. However, inevita-bly, owing to cultural and linguistic differences between languages, translations always fall short of this ideal. (1995:105)

The change in translation situations has called for a change in translator training:

> In order to teach prospective translators to produce accessible trans-lations, we need to be able to draw upon a particular type of framework

135

which is not dependent on rigid definitions of faithfulness, translation or text type and which is flexible enough to be used in any translation task that may arise, whether it be conventional translation or refor- mulation. (Walker et al. 1995:106)

'Accessibility' is the keyword in the new South African context. The gov- ernment, trade unions and banks have to communicate with the widest audience possible, including those with limited literacy. Some South Afri- can translation teachers have found that the functional approach is exactly what they need in these circumstances:

African-language translators are therefore now required to produce texts that are accessible to every level of society, even if this involves extensive rewriting of texts to ensure that they are understood by everyone. (Walker et al. 1995:102)

Glossary

Action: The process of acting, that is, of intentionally bringing about or preventing a change or transition from one state of affairs to another. See pp. 16-17 and Fig. 1, p. 18.

Adequacy: In terms of functional approaches to translation, 'adequacy' (German: 'Adäquatheit') is used to describe the appropriateness of a translated text for the communicative purpose defined in the translation brief. Adequacy is thus a dynamic concept related to the process of translational action. See pp. 34-37.

Appellative Function: The use of verbal or nonverbal communicative signs to obtain a certain response or reaction from the receiver. Also called 'operative' or 'conative' function (German: 'Appellfunktion'). Sub-functions: illustrative, persuasive, imperative, pedagogical, advertising, etc. The effectiveness of the appellative function depends on the receiver's susceptibility, sensitivity, previous experience and knowledge. See pp. 42-43, → *Function*.

Assignment: The commission given to a translator, including the working conditions (time, salary, etc.), the source text and (ideally) a translation brief. See p. 30; *assignment* in literary translation, see pp. 88-89.

Brief: Definition of the communicative purpose for which the translation is needed. The ideal brief provides explicit or implicit information about the intended target-text function(s), the target-text addressee(s), the medium over which it will be transmitted, the prospective place and time and, if necessary, motive of production or reception of the text. See pp. 30-31; 59-60.

Conventions: Implicit or tacit, non-binding regulations of behaviour, based on common knowledge and on the expectation of what others expect you to expect them (etc.) to do in a certain situation, e.g. text-type or genre conventions, general style conventions, measurement conventions, translation conventions. See pp. 53-59.

Cultureme: A social phenomenon of a culture A that is regarded as relevant by the members of this culture and, when compared with a corresponding social phenomenon in a culture B, is found to be specific to culture A. See p. 34.

Culture specificity: A culture-specific phenomenon is one that is found to exist – in this form or function – in only one of the two cultures being compared in the translation process. it does not mean that the phenomenon exists only in that particular culture. See p. 34.

Documentary Translation: Type of translation process which aims at producing in the target language a kind of document of (certain aspects of) a communicative interaction in which a source-culture sender communicates with a source-culture audience via the source text under source-culture conditions. According to which aspects of the source text are reproduced in the target text we distinguish interlineal, literal, philological and exoticizing documentary translations. See pp. 47-50.

Equivalence: A relationship of equal communicative value or function between a source and a target text or, on lower ranks, between words, phrases, sentences, syntactic structures etc. of a source and a target language (as in comparative linguistics). In terms of *Skopostheorie*, equivalence may be one possible aim when translating. See pp. 34-36.

Expressive Function: The use of verbal or nonverbal communicative signs to manifest a person's feelings or attitude towards the objects or phenomena of the world. It may be subdivided into sub-functions according to what is expressed, e.g. emotive or evaluative. If the expressive function is not marked explicitly, its comprehension relies on the existence of a common ground of shared values. Also 'emotive function' (German: 'Ausdrucksfunktion', 'expressive Funktion'). See p. 41.

Fidelity: → Intertextual coherence.

Function: The use a receiver makes of a text or the meaning that the text has for the receiver. In terms of *Skopostheorie*, the main guiding principle of the translation process. See pp. 27-29.

Functionalism: In translator training, methodological approach where the translator's decisions are governed by the intended function of the target text or any of its parts. The most important theory on which functionalism is based is the *Skopostheorie* developed by Hans J. Vermeer in 1978. See chapter 4.

Hypertext: A text, in whatever medium or media, that includes other texts. In conference interpreting, the conference can be regarded as a kind of hypertext of which the individual speeches and contributions by various speakers form a part. The *Skopos* of the interpretation has thus to be defined at the level of the conference assignment, whereas the function of individual sources can be perceived as a systemic variable in the communicative interplay of speakers and listeners physically co-present at a given place and time. See p. 107.

Initiator: The person or group of people or institution that starts off the translation process and determines its course by defining the purpose for which the target text is needed. Also 'commissioner' (German: 'Auftraggeber', 'Initiator'). See p. 20.

Instrumental Translation: A type of translation process which aims at producing in the target language an instrument for a new communicative interaction between the source-culture sender and a target-culture audience, using (certain aspects of) the source text as a model. According to the degree of functional invariance we may distinguish between equifunctional, heterofunctional and homologous instrumental translations. See pp. 50-52.

Intention: An aim-oriented plan of action on the part of either the sender or the receiver, pointing toward an appropriate way of producing or understanding the text. In Nord's terminology, 'intention' is defined from the sender's point of view, as 'intention to achieve a certain purpose with the text', whereas the receiver, before reception, has a certain kind of 'expectation' as to the meaning of the text. (German: 'Intention', 'Absicht'). See pp. 28-29.

Interpretation: The reader's elicitation of the sender's intention from the linguistic, stylistic and thematic markers exhibited in the text, seen in the light of any extratextual information about the sender and the situation-in-culture that may have guided the production of the text. See pp. 84-85.

Interpreting: Form of translational action, where the source text is presented only once, usually in oral form, and where the result of the translation process, however imperfect it may be, must be regarded as complete at the moment of text production. According to the presentation of the target text in relation to the source text we may distinguish simultaneous interpreting, consecutive interpreting, community interpreting, etc. See Fig. 1, p. 18, and pp. 104-105.

Intertextual Coherence: The relationship between the source and the target text within the framework of a *Skopos*-oriented translation (also 'fidelity'). The important point is that intertextual coherence should exist between source and target text, while the form it takes depends both on the translator's interpretation of the source text and on the translation *Skopos*. See p. 31-33.

Intratextual Coherence: In terms of *Skopostheorie*, the target text should be acceptable and meaningful in a sense that it is coherent with the situation in which it is received. Being 'coherent with' is synonymous with being 'part of' the receiver's situation and culture. See pp. 31-33.

Loyalty: The responsibility translators have toward their partners in translational interaction. Loyalty commits the translator bilaterally to the source and target sides, taking account of the the difference between culture-specific concepts of translation prevailing in the two cultures involved. See pp. 123-125.

Macrostructure: Structuring of a text into chapters, sections, paragraphs according to thematic or argumentative patterns. Some text-types or genres have a conventional macrostructure which may have to be adapted to target-culture standards in the translation process. See example pp. 57-58.

Phatic Function: The use of verbal and nonverbal communicative signs to establish, maintain or end contact between sender and receiver. The comprehension of the phatic function is based on the conventionality of the signs or sign combinations, as in salutations, small talk, introductory devices in tourist information texts etc. See pp. 44-45.

Purpose: Generally, the use for which a text or a translation is intended. In Vermeer's terminology, 'purpose' might also be used to translate the German term *Zweck*, a provisional stage in the process of attaining a *Ziel* or aim, which is then regarded as the final result of an action. See pp. 27-29.

Referential Function: The use of verbal and nonverbal signs to refer to the objects and phenomena of the world or of a particular world. According to the nature of the objects and phenomena we may distinguish various sub-functions, such as informative, metalinguistic, directive or didactic. The comprehension of the referential function relies on the existence of a sufficient amount of shared knowledge between sender and receiver. See p. 40-41.

Skopos: Greek for 'purpose'. According to *Skopostheorie*, the theory that applies the notion of *Skopos* to translation, the prime principle determining any translation process is the purpose (*Skopos*) of the overall translational action. See pp. 27-31.

Source Text (ST): The text that forms part of the translation assignment and has to be translated in the course of a translational action. A source text may consist of verbal and non-verbal elements (illustrations, plans, tables, charts, gestures, face and body movements, etc.). See p. 25; for *source-text analysis* in functional translation, see pp. 62-63.

Suprasegmental Features: All those features of text organization which overlap the boundaries of any lexical or syntactical segments, sentences, and paragraphs, framing the phonological 'gestalt' or specific 'tone' of the text. In spoken texts, suprasegmental features are signalled by acoustic means, such as tonicity, modulation, variations in pitch and loudness. In written texts, suprasegmental features are represented by rhythmical forms, focus structures or typographical means such as italics to indicate stress, etc. See examples pp. 101-103.

Target Text: The result of a translation process, also 'translated text' or 'translatum'. In terms of *Skopostheorie*, an offer of information formulated by a translator in a target culture and language about an offer of information formulated by someone else in a source culture and language. See pp. 31-32.

Text: Offer of information from which each receiver selects precisely those items that are interesting and important to them. See pp. 31-32.

Translation: In the wider sense, any translational action where a source text is transferred into a target culture and language. According to the form and presentation of the source text and to the correctibility of the target text we distinguish between oral translation (= 'interpreting') and written translation (= 'translation' in the narrower sense). See Fig. 1, p. 18.

Translational Action: Generic term coined by Justa Holz-Mänttäri in 1981 and designed to cover all forms of intercultural transfer, including those which do not involve any source or target texts. See pp. 12-13.

Translation Problem: Contrary to the translation difficulties encountered by an individual translator in their specific translation situation (for example, an unfamiliar word which is not in the dictionary), translation problems are regarded as the problems which have to be solved by the translator in the translation process in order to produce a functionally adequate target text and which can be verified objectively or at least intersubjectively. See pp. 64-68.

Translation Unit: The unit of verbal and/or nonverbal signs which cannot be broken down into smaller elements in the translation process. In linguistic approaches, translation units range from morpheme, word, phrase, sentence, paragraph to text. Functional approaches try to establish functional translation units. See pp. 68-73.

Bibliographical References

For easy reference, the basic texts and the works cited have been included in one alphabetical list. The main texts of 'Skopostheorie' and the functional approaches have been marked by an asterisk (*). Where appropriate, they are accompanied by an English translation of the title and a brief commentary in italics. All works have been listed under their first year of publication. If the page numbers cited in the text correspond to a translation or later edition, this has been indicated by giving the year of first publication in square brackets.

Agar, Michael (1991) 'The Biculture in Bilingual', *Language in Society* 20: 167-181.

Agar, Michael (1992) 'The Intercultural Frame', unpublished ms.

Albrecht, Jörn (1973) *Linguistik und Übersetzung*, Tübingen: Niemeyer.

Ameka, Felix K. (1994) 'Areal conversational routines and cross-cultural communication in a multilingual society', in Pürschel et al. (eds) *Intercultural Communication. Proceedings of the 17th International L.A.U.D. Symposium Duisburg 1992*, Frankfurt Main: Peter Lang, 441-469.

Ammann, Margret (1989a) '"Landeskunde" in der Translationsausbildung', *TEXTconTEXT* 4(1/2): 90-105.

Ammann, Margret (1989b) 'Fachkraft oder Mädchen für alles? – Funktion und Rolle des Translators als Dolmetscher und Begleiter ausländischer Delegationen', in Hans J. Vermeer (ed.) *Kulturspezifik des translatorischen Handelns*, Heidelberg: Institut für Übersetzen und Dolmetschen (= th – translatorisches handeln 3), 15-30.

Ammann, Margret (1989c) *Grundlagen der modernen Translationstheorie – Ein Leitfaden für Studierende*, Second Edition: Heidelberg: Institut für Übersetzen und Dolmetschen (= th – translatorisches handeln 1), 1990. *[Basic Aspects of Modern Translation Theory] A handbook for graduate students of university translator training in Germany.*

Ammann, Margret and Hans J. Vermeer (1990) *Entwurf eines Curriculums für einen Studiengang Translatologie und Translatorik*, Heidelberg: Institut für Übersetzen und Dolmetschen (= th – translatorisches handeln 4). *[Model for a Course in Translation Studies and Translator Training]*

Bakhtin, Mikhail (1990) *The Dialogic Imagination. Four Essays.* Trans. Caryl Emerson and Michael Holquist. Austin: University of Texas Press.

Bassnett, Susan and André Lefevere (eds) (1990) *Translation, History and Culture*. London & New York: Pinter.

Bassnett, Susan (1991) *Translation Studies*, Revised Edition, London & New York: Routledge.

Beaugrande, Robert A. and Wolfgang U. Dressler (1981) *Introduction to Text Linguistics*, London: Longman.

Beaugrande, Robert A. de (1978) *Factors in a Theory of Poetic Translation*, Assen (NL): Van Gorcum.

Beaugrande, Robert A. de (1980) *Text, Discourse and Process*, Norwood, NJ: Ablex.

Benjamin, Walter [1923] 'Die Aufgabe des Übersetzers', *Gesammelte Schriften*, vol. 1, Frankfurt a.M.: Suhrkamp. English version in *Illuminations*, translated by Harry Zohn, Harcourt Brace Jovanovich. Reproduced in Andrew Chesterman (ed), 13-24.

Berglund, Lars O. (1987) 'The Ethics of Ineffective Translation', *Lebende Sprachen* 32(1): 7-11.

Bochner, Stephen (1981) 'The Social Psychology of Cultural Mediation', in Stephen Bochner (ed) *The Mediating Person: Bridges between Cultures*, Cambridge Mass.: G. K. Hall, 7-36.

Broeck, Raymond van den (1980) 'Toward a text-type-oriented theory of translation', in Sven-Olaf Poulsen and Wolfram Wilss (eds) *Angewandte Übersetzungswissenschaft*, Aarhus: Aarhus Business School, 82-96.

Bühler, Karl (1934) *Sprachtheorie*, Jena: Fischer.

Catford, J. C. (1965) *A Linguistic Theory of Translation*, London: Oxford University Press.

Chesterman, Andrew (1993) 'From "Is" to "Ought": Laws, Norms and Strategies in Translation Studies', *Target* 5(1): 1-20.

Chesterman, Andrew (ed.) (1989) *Readings in Translation*, Helsinki: Oy Finn Lectura Ab.

Chomsky, Noam (1957) *Syntactic Structures*, The Hague: Mouton.

Chomsky, Noam (1965) *Aspects of the Theory of Syntax*, Cambridge Mass.: MIT Press.

Cicero, Marcus Tullius [46 B.C.E] *De optimo genere oratorum*, English translation by H. M. Hubbell, London: Heinemann, 1959 (= Loeb Classical Library).

Coseriu, Eugenio (1971) 'Thesen zum Thema Sprache und Dichtung', in Wolf-Dieter Stempel (ed) *Beiträge zur Textlinguistik*, München: Fink, 183-188.

Dedecius, Karl (1986) *Vom Übersetzen*, Frankfurt a.M.: Suhrkamp.

Delabastita, Dirk (1989) 'Translation and mass-communication: film and T.V. translation as evidence of cultural dynamics', *Babel* 35(4): 193-218.

Dijk, Teun A. Van (1972) *Some Aspects of Text Grammar*, The Hague: Mouton.

Diller, H. J. and J. Kornelius (1978) *Linguistische Probleme der Übersetzung*, Tübingen: Niemeyer.

Dollerup, Cay and Anne Loddegaard (eds) (1992) *Teaching Translation and Interpreting 1. Training, Talent and Experience*, Amsterdam & Philadelphia: Benjamins.

Dollerup, Cay and Annette Lindegaard (eds) (1994) *Teaching Translation and Interpreting 2*, Amsterdam & Philadelphia: Benjamins.

Even-Zohar, Itamar (1975) 'Decisions in Translating Poetry', *Ha-sifrut/Literature* 21: 32-45 (Hebrew).

Fitts, D. [1959] 'The poetic nuance', in Ruben A. Brower (ed) *On Translation*, Cambridge Mass.: Harvard University Press. Second edition: New York: Oxford University Press, 32-47.

Freihoff, Roland (1991) 'Funktionalität und Kreativität im Translationsprozeß',

Erikoiskielet ja käännösteoria (LSP and Translation Theory). VAKKI-Seminaari XI, Vaasa: Vaasa University, 36-45.

Friedrich, Hugo (1965) *Zur Frage der Übersetzungskunst*, Heidelberg: Akademie der Wissenschaft.

Gentzler, Edwin (1993) *Contemporary Translation Theories*, London & New York: Routledge.

Gerzymisch-Arbogast, Heidrun (1994) *Übersetzungswissenschaftliches Propädeutikum*, Tübingen & Basel: Francke (= UTB 1782).

Göhring, Heinz (1978) 'Interkulturelle Kommunikation: Die Überwindung der Trennung von Fremdsprachen- und Landeskundeunterricht durch einen integrierten Fremdverhaltensunterricht', in Matthias Hartig (ed) *Soziolinguistik, Psycholinguistik. Kongreßberichte der 8. Jahrestagung der Gesellschaft für Angewandte Linguistik*. Vol. 4. Stuttgart: Hochschulverlag, 9-14.

Goodenough, Ward H. (1964) 'Cultural Anthropology and Linguistics', in Dell Hymes (ed) *Language in Culture and Society: A Reader in Linguistics and Anthropology*, New York: Harper & Row, 36-40.

Göpferich, Susanne (1995a) *Textsorten in Naturwissenschaft und Technik: Pragmatische Typologie – Kontrastierung – Translation*. Tübingen: Narr (= Forum für Fachsprachenforschung 27).

Göpferich, Susanne (1995b) 'A Pragmatic Classification of LSP Texts in Science and Technology', *Target* 7(2): 305-326.

Grabes, Herbert (1977) 'Fiktion – Realismus – Ästhetik. Woran erkennt der Leser Literatur?' in Herbert Grabes (ed) *Text – Leser – Bedeutung*, Grossen-Linden: Hoffmann, 61-81.

Harras, Gisela (1978) *Kommunikative Handlungstexte, oder: Eine Möglichkeit, Handlungsabfolgen als Zusammenhänge zu erklären, exemplarisch an Theatertexten*, Tübingen: Niemeyer (= Reihe Germanistische Linguistik 16).

Hartmann, Peter (1970) 'Übersetzen als Thema im linguistischen Aufgabenbereich', in Hartmann and Vernay (eds), 12-32.

Hartmann, Peter and Henri Vernay (eds) (1970) *Sprachwissenschaft und Übersetzen. Symposium an der Universität Heidelberg 24.2.-26.2.1969*, Munich: Hueber.

Hermans, Theo (1985) 'Translation Studies and a New Paradigm', in Theo Hermans (ed) *The Manipulation of Literature. Studies in Literary Translation*, London: Croom Helm, 7-15.

Hewson, Lance and Jacky Martin (1991) *Redefining Translation*, London & New York: Routledge.

Hofstede, G. (1980) *Culture's Consequences: International Differences in Work-related Values*, Beverly Hills CA: Sage.

Holmes, James S. (1988) *Translated!*, Amsterdam & Atlanta: Rodopi.

Holz-Mänttäri, Justa (1981) 'Übersetzen – Theoretischer Ansatz und Konsequenzen für die Ausbildung', *Kääntäjä/Översättaren* 24: 2-3.

*Holz-Mänttäri, Justa (1984a) *Translatorisches Handeln. Theorie und Methode*, Helsinki: Suomalainen Tiedeakatemia (= Annales Academiae Scientiarum Fennicae B 226). [*Translational Action: Theory and Method. Systematic rep-*

resentation of an action-based model of 'translation' in a very broad sense. Translational action is conceived as a process in which an agent (= the translator) produces 'message transmitters' (= 'texts' consisting of verbal and non-verbal components) which can be used by other agents (e.g. the initiator, the target receivers) in their communicative and non-communicative interactions for various purposes.

Holz-Mänttäri, Justa (1984b) 'Sichtbarmachung und Beurteilung translatorischer Leistungen bei der Ausbildung von Berufstranslatoren', in Wolfram Wilss and Gisela Thome (eds) *Die Theorie des Übersetzens und ihr Aufschlußwert für die Übersetzungs- und Dolmetschdidaktik. Akten des Internationalen Kolloquiums der AILA – Saarbrücken 1983*, Tübingen: Narr (= Tübinger Beiträge zur Linguistik 247), 176-185.

Holz-Mänttäri, Justa (1984c) 'Die Produktbeschreibung im Werkvertrag des Profi-Übersetzers', *Kääntäjä Översättaren* 3: 4-7.

Holz-Mänttäri, Justa (1986b) 'Translatorische Fort- und Weiterbildung – Ein Organisationsmodell', *TEXTconTEXT* 1: 75-95; extended version (also in German) in Yves Gambier (ed) *Trans*, Turku: Turku University, 1988, 70-117.

Holz-Mänttäri, Justa (1988a) 'Texter von Beruf', *TEXTconTEXT* 3: 153-173.

Holz-Mänttäri, Justa (ed) (1988b) *Translationstheorie – Grundlagen und Standorte*, Tampere: Tampere University (= studia translatologica A 1).

Holz-Mänttäri, Justa (1988c) 'Translation und das biologisch-soziale Gefüge "Mensch"', in Holz-Mänttäri 1988b, 39-57.

Holz-Mänttäri, Justa (1989) 'Denkmodelle für die Aus- und Weiterbildung auf dem Prüfstand der Praxis', *Mitteilungsblatt für Dolmetscher und Übersetzer* 35: 3-7.

Holz-Mänttäri, Justa (1993) 'Textdesign – verantwortlich und gehirngerecht,' in Holz-Mänttäri and Nord (eds), 301-320.

Holz-Mänttäri, Justa and Hans J. Vermeer (1985) 'Entwurf für einen Studiengang Translatorik und einen Promotionsstudiengang Translatologie', *Kääntäjä/Översättaren* 3: 4-6. *[A Model for a Graduate Course in Translation and a Postgraduate Course in Translation Studies]*

Holz-Mänttäri, Justa and Christiane Nord (eds) (1993) *Traducere navem. Festschrift für Katharina Reiss zum 70. Geburtstag*, Tampere: University (= studia translatologica A 3).

Hönig, Hans G. (1987) 'Wer macht die Fehler?' in J. Albrecht et al. (eds) *Translation und interkulturelle Kommunikation*, Frankfurt a.M.: Peter Lang, 37-46.

Hönig, Hans G. (1993) 'Vom Selbst-Bewußtsein des Übersetzers', in Holz-Mänttäri and Nord (eds), 77-90.

Hönig, Hans G. (1995) *Konstruktives Übersetzen*, Tübingen: Stauffenburg (= Studien zur Translation 1).

Hönig, Hans G. and Paul Kussmaul (1982) *Strategie der Übersetzung. Ein Lehr- und Arbeitsbuch*, Tübingen: Narr.

Horace [20 B.C.E], *Ars poetica I:33 – On the Art of Poetry*, English translation by T. S. Dorsch in *Classical Literary Criticism*, Harmondsworth: Penguin, 1965, 79-95.

House, Juliane (1977) *A Model for Translation Quality Assessment*, Second Edition, Tübingen: Narr, 1981.

Hulst, Jacqueline (1995) *De doeltekst centraal. Naar een functioneel model voor vertaalkritiek*, Amsterdam: Thesis Publishers (= Perspektieven op taalkritiek).

Irmen, Friedrich (1970) 'Bedeutungsumfang und Bedeutung im Übersetzungsprozeß', in Hartmann and Vernay (eds), 144-156.

Jakobsen, Arnt Lykke (1993) 'Translation as textual (re)production', in Holz-Mänttäri and Nord (eds), 66-76.

Jakobsen, Arnt Lykke (1994a) 'Starting from the (other) end: integrating translation and text production', in Dollerup and Lindegaard (eds), 143-156.

Jakobsen, Arnt Lykke (1994b) 'Translation – A Productive Skill,' in Henning Bergenholtz et al. (eds) *Translating LSP Texts. Conference Papers of the OFT Symposium, Copenhagen Business School April 1994*, Copenhagen: Copenhagen Business School, 41-70.

Jakobson, Roman (1960) 'Linguistics and Poetics', in Thomas A. Sebeok (ed) *Style in Language*. Cambridge Mass.: MIT Press, 350-377.

Kade, Otto (1968) *Zufall und Gesetzmäßigkeit in der Übersetzung*, Leipzig: VEB Enzyklopädie.

Kelly, Louis G. (1979) *The True Interpreter. A History of Translation Theory and Practice in the West*, Oxford: Basil Blackwell.

Koller, Werner [1979] *Einführung in die Übersetzungswissenschaft*, Heidelberg: Quelle & Meyer; English translation of a chapter in Chesterman (ed), 99-104.

Koller, Werner (1992) *Einführung in die Übersetzungswissenschaft*, 4th edition, totally revised, Heidelberg: Quelle & Meyer.

Koller, Werner (1993) 'Zum Begriff der "eigentlichen" Übersetzung', in Holz-Mänttäri and Nord (eds), 49-64.

Koller, Werner (1995) 'The Concept of Equivalence and the Object of Translation Studies', *Target* 7(2): 191-222.

Königs, Frank G. (1981) 'Zur Frage der Übersetzungseinheit und ihre Relevanz für den Fremdsprachenunterricht', *Linguistische Berichte* 74: 82-103.

Kroeber, A.L. and Clyde Kluckhohn (1966) *Culture: A Critical Review of Concepts and Definitions*, New York: Vintage.

Kupsch-Losereit, Sigrid (1985) 'The problem of translation error evaluation', in Christopher Tietford and A. E. Hieke (eds) *Translation in Foreign Language Teaching and Testing*, Tübingen: Narr, 169-179.

Kupsch-Losereit, Sigrid (1986) 'Scheint eine schöne Sonne? oder: Was ist ein Übersetzungsfehler?', *Lebende Sprachen* 31(1): 12-16.

Kussmaul, Paul (1993) 'Empirische Grundlagen einer Übersetzungsdidaktik: Kreativität im Übersetzungsprozeß', in Holz-Mänttäri and Nord (eds), 275-288.

Kussmaul, Paul (1995) *Training the Translator*, Amsterdam & Philadelphia: Benjamins.

Larose, Robert (1989) *Théories contemporaines de la traduction*, Second edition: Québec: Presses de l'Université du Québec, 1992.

146

Löwe, Barbara (1989) 'Funktionsgerechte Kulturkompetenz von Translatoren: Desiderata an eine universitäre Ausbildung (am Beispiel des Russischen)', in Vermeer (ed) (1989), 89-111.

Luther, Martin [1530] 'Sendbrief vom Dolmetschen', reproduced in Hans-Joachim Störig (ed) *Das Problem des Übersetzens*, Darmstadt: Wiss. Buchgesellschaft, 1963.

Mauranen, Anna (1993) *Cultural Differences in Academic Rhetoric. A Text Linguistic Study*, Frankfurt a.M. etc.: Peter Lang (= Scandinavian University Studies in the Humanities and Social Sciences 4).

Neubert, Albrecht (1973) 'Invarianz und Pragmatik', in: Albrecht Neubert and Otto Kade (eds) *Neue Beiträge zu Grundfragen der Übersetzungswissenschaft*, Leipzig: Enzyklopädie, 13-25.

Newmark, Peter (1984-85) 'Literal Translation', *Parallèles* 7: 11-19.

Newmark, Peter (1990) 'The Curse of Dogma in Translation Studies', *Lebende Sprachen* 35(3): 105-108.

Nida, Eugene A. (1964) *Toward a Science of Translating. With special reference to principles and procedures involved in Bible translating*, Leiden: Brill.

Nida, Eugene A. (1969) 'Science of Translation', *Language* 45: 483-498.

Nida, Eugene A. (1976) 'A Framework for the Analysis and Evaluation of Theories of Translation', in Richard W. Brislin (ed) *Translation. Application and Research*, New York: Gardner Press, 47-91.

Nida, Eugene A. and Charles Taber (1969) *The Theory and Practice of Translation*, Leiden: Brill.

Nord, Christiane (1987) 'Übersetzungsprobleme – Übersetzungsschwierigkeiten. Was in den Köpfen von Übersetzern vorgehen sollte...', *Mitteilungsblatt für Dolmetscher und Übersetzer* 2: 5-8.

*Nord, Christiane (1988a) *Textanalyse und Übersetzen. Theorie, Methode und didaktische Anwendung einer übersetzungsrelevanten Textanalyse*, Revised edition, Heidelberg: Groos, 1991. Third edition 1995. English version 1991: *Text Analysis in Translation. Theory, Methodology, and Didactic Application of a Model for Translation-Oriented Text Analysis*, Amsterdam & Atlanta: Rodopi. *A pedagogical model for a functional analysis of both the source-text and the target-text profile as defined by the translation brief, which serves to identify pragmatic, cultural and linguistic translation problems. Discussion of didactic aspects of text selection, learning progression, and evaluation in translation classes, with many examples, mainly from Spanish, English and German.*

*Nord, Christiane (1988b) 'Übersetzungshandwerk – Übersetzungskunst. Was bringt die Translationstheorie für das literarische Übersetzen?', *Lebende Sprachen* 33(2): 51-57. *[Translation as a Craft or an Art. What is the use of theory in literary translation?] A first attempt to apply modern functionalist translation theory to the translation of literary texts (see chapter 5).*

*Nord, Christiane (1989) 'Loyalität statt Treue', *Lebende Sprachen* 34(3): 100-105. *[Loyalty instead of Fidelity. Suggestions for a Functional Typology of Translations]. See chapter 4.*

*Nord, Christiane (1990-91) *Übersetzen lernen - leicht gemacht. Kurs zur Einführung in das professionelle Übersetzen Spanisch-Deutsch*, Heidelberg: Institut für Übersetzen und Dolmetschen (= th - translatorisches handeln 5). *[Teach Yourself Translation. Introduction to Professional Translating from Spanish into German]. A collection of Spanish source texts, didactic explanations, German parallel texts, a systematic analysis and discussion of translation problems from a functionalist perspective.*

Nord, Christiane (1991) 'Scopos, Loyalty and Translational Conventions', *Target* 3(1): 91-109.

Nord, Christiane (1992a) 'Text Analysis in Translator Training', in Cay Dollerup and Anne Loddegaard (eds) *Teaching Translation and Interpreting. Selected Papers of the First Language International Conference, Elsinore 1991*. Amsterdam & Philadelphia: Benjamins, 39-48.

Nord, Christiane (1992b) 'The Relationship between Text Function and Meaning in Translation', in Barbara Lewandowska-Tomaszcyk and Marcel Thelen (eds) *Translation and Meaning, Part 2*, Maastricht: Rijkshogeschool Maastricht, Faculty of Translation and Interpreting, 91-96.

*Nord, Christiane (1993) *Einführung in das funktionale Übersetzen. Am Beispiel von Titeln und Überschriften*, Tübingen: Francke (=UTB 1734). *[Introduction to Functional Translation. Titles and Headings as a Case in Point] Book titles and text headings are regarded as a useful paradigm for the justification and application of a functionalist approach to translation. Using a corpus of more than 12,500 items, the author analyzes the formal and functional text-type conventions of English, Spanish, French and German titles, which then serve as a basis for the comparison and evaluation of a large number of title translations on functional grounds.*

Nord, Christiane (1994a) 'It's Tea-Time in Wonderland: culture-markers in fictional texts', in Heiner Pürschel et al. (eds), 523-538.

Nord, Christiane (1994b) 'Aus Fehlern lernen: Überlegungen zur Beurteilung von Übersetzungsleistungen', in Mary Snell-Hornby et al. (eds), 363-375.

Nord, Christiane (1995) 'Text Functions in Translation. Titles and Headings as a Case in Point', *Target* 7(2): 261-284. *A brief summary of the main ideas in Nord 1993.*

Nord, Christiane (1996a) '"Wer nimmt denn mal den ersten Satz?" Überlegungen zu neuen Arbeitsformen im Übersetzungsunterricht', in Angelika Lauer et al. (eds) *Übersetzungswissenschaft im Umbruch. Festschrift für Wolfram Wilss zum 70. Geburtstag*, Tübingen: Narr, 313-327.

Nord, Christiane (1996b) 'Revisiting the Classics – Text Type and Translation Method. An Objective Approach to Translation Criticism', Review of Katharina Reiss's *Möglichkeiten und Grenzen der Übersetzungskritik*, *The Translator* 2(1): 81-88.

Nord, Christiane (1996c) 'El error en la traducción: categorías y evaluación', in Amparo Hurtado Albir (ed) *La enseñanza de la traducción*, Castelló: Universitat Jaume I, 91-107.

Nord, Christiane (1997a) 'Alice abroad. Dealing with descriptions and transcriptions of paralanguage in literary translation', in Fernando Poyatos (ed) *Nonverbal Communication in Translation: Theoretical and Methodological Perspectives*, Amsterdam & Philadelphia: Benjamins.

Nord, Christiane (1997b) 'Vertikal statt horizontal. Die Frage der Übersetzungeinheit aus funktionaler Sicht', in Peter Holzer and Cornelia Feyrer (eds) *Text, Kultur, Kommunikation*, Frankfurt a.M. etc.: Peter Lang.

Nord, Christiane (1997c) 'A Functional Typology of Translations', in Anna Trosborg (ed) *Scope and Skopos in Translation*, Amsterdam & Philadelphia: Benjamins.

Oettinger, Anthony G. (1960) *Automatic Language Translation. Lexical and Technical Aspects, with Particular Reference to Russian*, Cambridge Mass.: Harvard University Press.

Oittinen, Riitta (1990) 'The dialogic relation between text and illustration: a translatological view', *TEXTconTEXT* 5(1): 40-53.

Oittinen, Riitta (1993) *I Am Me – I Am Other: On the Dialogics of Translating for Children*, Tampere: University of Tampere.

Oittinen, Riitta (1995) 'Translating and Reading Experience', in Oittinen and Varonen (eds), 17-31.

Oittinen, Riitta and Jukka-Pekka Varonen (eds) (1995) *Aspectus varii translationis*, Tampere: University of Tampere.

Poulsen, Sven-Olaf and Wolfram Wilss (eds) (1980) *Angewandte Übersetzungswissenschaft. Internationales übersetzungswissenschaftliches Kolloquium an der Wirtschaftsuniversität Aarhus/Danmark 1980*, Aarhus: Aarhus Business School.

Pöchhacker, Franz (1992) 'The Role of Theory in Simultaneous Interpreting', in Dollerup and Loddegaard (eds), 211-220.

Pöchhacker, Franz (1994a) *Simultandolmetschen als komplexes Handeln*, Tübingen: Narr (= Language in Performance, 10).

Pöchhacker, Franz (1994b) 'Simultaneous interpretation: "Cultural transfer" or "voice-over text"?' in Mary Snell-Hornby et al. (eds), 169-178.

Pöchhacker, Franz (1995) 'Simultaneous Interpreting: A Functionalist Perspective', *Hermes, Journal of Linguistics* 14: 31-53.

Pürschel, Heiner et al. (eds) *Intercultural Communication.Proceedings of the 17th International L.A.U.D, Symposium Duisburg 1992*, Frankfurt a.M. etc.: Peter Lang

Pym, Anthony (1992a) *Translation and Text Transfer. An Essay on the Principles of Intercultural Communication*, Frankfurt a.M. etc.: Peter Lang.

Pym, Anthony (1992b) 'Translation Error Analysis and the Interface with Language Teaching', in Dollerup and Loddegaard (eds), 279-288.

Pym, Anthony (1993a) 'Why translation conventions should be intercultural rather than culture-specific. An alternative basic-link model', *Parallèles* 15: 60-68.

Pym, Anthony (1993b) 'Coming to terms with and against nationalist cultural specificity. Notes for an ethos of translation studies', in Jana Králova and Zuzana Jettmarová (eds), *Folia Translatologica*, Prague: Charles University, 49-69.

Pym, Anthony (1996) 'Material Text Transfer as a Key to the Purposes of Translation', in Albrecht Neubert, Gregory Shreve and Klaus Gommlich (eds), *Basic Issues in Translation Studies. Proceedings of the Fifth International Conference Kent Forum on Translation Studies II*, Kent, Ohio: Institute of Applied Linguistics, 337-346.

Rehbein, Jochen (1977) *Komplexes Handeln. Elemente zur Handlungstheorie der Sprache*, Stuttgart: Metzler.

*Reiss, Katharina (1971) *Möglichkeiten und Grenzen der Übersetzungskritik. Kategorien und Kriterien für eine sachgerechte Beurteilung von Übersetzungen*, Munich: Hueber. *[Possibilities and Limitations of Translation Criticism. Categories and Criteria for a Fair Evaluation of Translations]. The first presentation of Reiss's translation-oriented text typology, based on Karl Bühler's organon model of langage functions. For a detailed review see Nord 1996b.*

Reiss, Katharina (1976) *Texttyp und Übersetzungsmethode. Der operative Text*, Kronberg: Scriptor; Second edition: Heidelberg: Julius Groos, 1983. *[Text Type and Translation Method. Operative Texts]. An elaboration of the 1971 model, applied to the translation of operative texts.*

*Reiss, Katharina [1977] 'Texttypen, Übersetzungstypen und die Beurteilung von Übersetzungen', *Lebende Sprachen* 22(3): 97-100. English Translation as 'Text types, translation types and translation assessment', in Chesterman (ed), 105-115.

*Reiss, Katharina [1983] 'Adequacy and Equivalence in Translation', *The Bible Translator* (Technical Papers), 3: 301-208. German version as 'Adäquatheit und Äquivalenz', in Wolfram Wilss and Gisela Thome (eds), 80-89. Elaborated German version as 'Adäquatheit und Äquivalenz', *Hermes. Journal of Linguistics* 3 (1989): 161-177.

Reiss, Katharina (1986) 'Ortega y Gasset, die Sprachwissenschaft und das Übersetzen', *Babel* 32(4): 202-214.

Reiss, Katharina (1987) 'Pragmatic Aspects of Translation', *Indian Journal of Applied Linguistics* 13(2): 47-59.

Reiss, Katharina (1988) '"Der" Text und der Übersetzer', in Reiner Arntz (ed) *Textlinguistik und Fachsprache*, Hildesheim: Olms, 67-75.

*Reiss, Katharina and Hans J. Vermeer (1984) *Grundlegung einer allgemeinen Translationstheorie*, Tübingen: Niemeyer. Abridged translation into Finnish by P. Roinila, Helsinki: Gaudeamus 1985. Translation into Spanish by Celia Martín de León and Sandra García Reina, *Fundamentos para una teoría funcional de la traducción*, Madrid: Akal, 1996. *[Groundwork for a General Theory of Translation] The first part, by Vermeer, presents the basic principles of 'Skopostheorie' as a general action-oriented theory of translation and interpreting. The second part, by Katharina Reiss, focuses on a 'specific' theory integrating Reiss's text typology into the framework of functionalism. 'Specific' refers to the special case where the translation purpose demands invariance of function with regard to the source text.*

Risku, Hanna (1995) 'Verstehen im Translationsprozeß', in Oittinen and Varonen (eds), 33-46.

Sager, Juan C. (1983) 'Quality and Standards – the Evaluation of Translations', in Catriona Picken (ed) *The Translator's Handbook*, London: Aslib, 121-128.

Sager, Juan C. (1993) *Language Engineering and Translation. Consequences of Automation*, Amsterdam & Philadelphia: Benjamins.

Schmidt, Siegfried J. (1970) 'Text und Bedeutung', in Siegfried J. Schmidt (ed) *Text, Bedeutung, Ästhetik*, Munich: Bayerischer Schulbuch-Verlag, 43-49.

Schmitt, Peter A. (1989) 'Kulturspezifik von Technik-Texten: Ein translatorisches und terminographisches Problem', in Vermeer (ed), 53-87.

Schopp, Jürgen (1995) 'Typographie und Layout im Translationsprozeß', in Oittinen and Varonen (eds), 59-78.

Searle, John (1969) *Speech acts. An Essay in the Philosophy of Language*, London. Cambridge University Press.

Snell-Hornby, Mary (ed) (1986) *Übersetzungswissenschaft – eine Neuorientierung. Zur Integrierung von Theorie und Praxis*, Tübingen: Narr (= UTB 1415).

Snell-Hornby, Mary (1987) 'Translation as a Cross-Cultural Event: Midnight's Children – Mitternachtskinder', *Indian Journal of Applied Linguistics* 13(2): 91-105.

Snell-Hornby, Mary (1988) *Translation Studies: An Integrated Approach*, Amsterdam & Philadelphia: Benjamins.

Snell-Hornby, Mary (1990) 'Linguistic Transcoding or Cultural Transfer? A Critique of Translation Theory in Germany', in Bassnett and Lefevere (eds), 79-86.

Snell-Hornby, Mary, Franz Pöchhacker and Klaus Kaindl (eds) *Translation Studies – An Interdiscipline*, Amsterdam & Philadelphia: Benjamins.

Steiner, George (1972) *On Difficulty and Other Essays*. Reprint: Oxford: Oxford University Press, 1978.

Stellbrink, Hans-Jürgen (1987) 'Der Übersetzer und Dolmetscher beim Abschluß internationaler Verträge', *TEXTconTEXT* 2(1): 32-41.

Stolze, Radegundis (1982) *Grundlagen der Textübersetzung*, Heidelberg: Groos.

Toury, Gideon (1980a) *In Search of a Theory of Translation*, Tel Aviv: The Porter Institute for Poetics and Semiotics, Tel Aviv University.

Toury, Gideon (1980b) 'The Translator as a Nonconformist-to-be, or: How to Train Translators So As to Violate Translational Norms', in Poulsen and Wilss (eds), 180-194.

Toury, Gideon (1995) *Descriptive Translation Studies and Beyond*, Amsterdam & Philadelphia: Benjamins.

Vermeer, Hans J. (1972) *Allgemeine Sprachwissenschaft. Eine Einführung*, Freiburg: Rombach.

Vermeer, Hans J. (1976) Review of 'La Traduzione. Saggi e studi', *Göttingische Gelehrte Anzeigen* 228: 147-162.

*Vermeer, Hans J. (1978) Ein Rahmen für eine allgemeine Translationstheorie, *Lebende Sprachen* 23(1): 99-102. Reprinted in Vermeer 1983, 48-88. *[A Framework for a General Theory of Translation] First publication of the basic principles and rules of 'Skopostheorie': translation as a subcategory of* intercultural interaction, 'Skopos' rule, coherence rule, fidelity rule in a hierarchical order.

*Vermeer, Hans J. (1979) Vom 'richtigen' Übersetzen. *Mitteilungsblatt für Dolmetscher und Übersetzer* 25.4, 2-8. Reprinted in Vermeer (ed) 1983, 62-88. *[How to translate 'correctly'].* Analysis and discussion of the concepts 'invariance of function' and 'invariance of effect'.

*Vermeer, Hans J. (1982) 'Translation als "Informationsangebot"', *Lebende Sprachen* 27(2): 97-101.

Vermeer, Hans J. (1983a) 'Translation theory and linguistics', in Pauli Roinila, Ritva Orfanos, and Sonja Tirkkonen-Condit (eds) *Näkökohtia käänämisen tutkimuksesta.* Joensuu (= Joensuun kokeakoulu, kielten osaston ulkaisuja 10), 1-10.

Vermeer, Hans J. (1983b) *Aufsätze zur Translationstheorie*, Heidelberg (Reprints of articles on *Skopostheorie* published earlier in various journals, including Vermeer 1978, 1979).

Vermeer, Hans J. (1983c) 'Modell einiger Kommunikationsfaktoren', in Vermeer 1983b, 39-45.

Vermeer, Hans J. (1985) Was dolmetscht der Dolmetscher, wenn er dolmetscht, in Rehbein, Jochen (ed.) *Interkulturelle Kommunikation*, Tübingen: Narr (= Kommunikation und Institution 12), 475-482.

*Vermeer, Hans J. (1986a) *voraus-setzungen für eine translationstheorie. einige kapitel kultur- und sprachtheorie*, Heidelberg: Vermeer. *[Pre-suppositions for a theory of translation. Some theoretical considerations on culture and language]* Explication of Vermeer's 'cultural relativism', sign theory, conceptions of culture, behaviour, enculturation, cooperation. Draft of a theory of action. The application of Grice's conversational maxims to translation. Theories of text reception (i.e. relativization of the source text) and text production.

Vermeer, Hans J. (1986b) 'Betrifft: Dolmetschausbildung', *TEXTconTEXT* 1(4): 234-248.

Vermeer, Hans J. (1986c) 'Übersetzen als kultureller Transfer', in Snell-Hornby (ed), 30-53.

Vermeer, Hans J. (1986d) 'Naseweise Bemerkungen zum literarischen Übersetzen', *TEXTconTEXT* 1(3): 145-150.

Vermeer, Hans J. (1987a) 'What does it mean to translate?' *Indian Journal of Applied Linguistics* 13(2): 25-33.

Vermeer, Hans J. (1987b) 'Literarische Übersetzung als Versuch interkultureller Kommunikation', in Alois Wierlacher (ed) *Perspektiven und Verfahren interkultureller Germanistik*, München: Iudicium (= Publikationen der Gesellschaft für interkulturelle Germanistik 3), 541-549. *[Literary Translation as an Attempt at Intercultural Communication]*

Vermeer, Hans J. (1988) 'From Cicero to Modern Times - Rhetorics and Translation', in Holz-Mänttäri (ed), 93-128.

*Vermeer, Hans J. (1989a) *Skopos und Translationsauftrag – Aufsätze.* Heidelberg: Universität (thw – translatorisches handeln wissenschaft 2), Second edition 1990. *[Skopos and Translation Commission], elaborated version of Vermeer 1989b, see below.*

*Vermeer, Hans J. (1989b) 'Skopos and commission in translational action', in Chesterman (ed), 173-187. *Article specially written for the volume, outlining two central concepts in the theory of translational action: the 'Skopos' and the commission or translation brief (see chapter 3).*

Vermeer, Hans J. (ed.) (1989c) *Kulturspezifik des translatorischen Handelns*, Heidelberg: Institut für Übersetzen und Dolmetschen (= th – translatorisches handeln 3).

Vermeer, Hans J. (1990a) '"Funktionskonstanz" und "tertium comparationis". Zu zwei Begriffen der Translationstheorie', in Gebhard Fürst (ed) *Gottes Wort in der Sprache der Zeit. 10 Jahre Einheitsübersetzung der Bibel*, Stuttgart: Akademie der Diözese Rottenburg-Stuttgart (= Hohenheimer Protokolle 35), 39-42.

Vermeer, Hans J. (1990b) 'Quality in Translation - a social task', *The CERA Lectures 1990*. The CERA Chair for Translation, Communication and Cultures, Katholieke Universiteit Leuven, Belgium, June/July 1990 [ms.]

Vermeer, Hans J. (1992) 'Describing Nonverbal Behavior in the Odyssey: Scenes and Verbal Frames as Translation Problems', in Fernando Poyatos (ed) *Advances in Nonverbal Communication. Sociocultural, Clinical, Esthetic and Literary Perspectives*, Amsterdam & Philadelphia: Benjamins, 285-299.

*Vermeer, Hans J. and Heidrun Witte (1990) *Mögen Sie Zistrosen? Scenes & frames & channels im translatorischen Handeln*, Heidelberg: Groos (= TEXTconTEXT Beiheft 3). *Application of the concepts 'scene', 'frame' and 'channel' to translation.*

Vermeer, Manuel (1989) 'Fremde Teufel und blaue Ameisen' – Vom Einfluß der Mentalitätsproblematik beim Dolmetschen Chinesisch-Deutsch und Deutsch-Chinesisch, in Vermeer (ed), 31-48.

Vernay, Henri (1970) 'Zur semantischen Struktur des Verbalknotens und des Nominalknotens', in Hartmann and Vernay (eds), 93-103.

Vinay, J.-P. and Jean Darbelnet (1958) *Stylistique comparée du français et de l'anglais. Méthode de traduction*, Paris: Didier.

Vuorinen, Erkka (1995) 'Source Text Status and (News) Translation', in Oittinen and Varonen (eds), 89-102.

Walker, A. K., Alet Kruger, and I. C. Andrews (1995) 'Translation as Transformation: A Process of Linguistic and Cultural Adaptation', *South African Journal of Linguistics*, Suppl. 26: 99-115.

Watzlawick, Paul, Janet H. Beavin and Don D. Jackson (eds) (1972) *Menschliche Kommunikation. Formen, Störungen, Paradoxien*, Stuttgart: Huber.

Wilss, Wolfram (1977) *Übersetzungswissenschaft. Probleme und Methoden*, Tübingen: Narr; English translation as *Translation Science. Problems and Methods*, Tübingen: Narr, 1982.

Wilss, Wolfram, and Gisela Thome (eds) (1984) *Die Theorie des Übersetzens und ihr Aufschlußwert für die Übersetzungs- und Dolmetschdidaktik – Translation Theory and its Implementation in the Teaching of Translating and Interpreting. Akten des Internationalen Kolloquiums der AILA – Saarbrücken 1983*, Tübingen: Narr (= Tübinger Beiträge zur Linguistik 247).

Witte, Heidrun (1987) 'Die Kulturkompetenz des Translators – Theoretisch-abstrakter Begriff oder realisierbares Konzept?', *TEXTconTEXT* 2(2): 109-137.

Witte, Heidrun (1992) 'Zur gesellschaftlichen Verantwortung des Translators – Anmerkungen', *TEXTconTEXT* 7(2): 119-129.

Witte, Heidrun (1994) 'Translation as a means for a better understanding between cultures?', in Dollerup and Lindegaard (eds), 69-75.

Wright, Georg Henrik (1963) *Norm and Action. A Logical Enquiry*, London: Routledge & Kegan Paul (= International Library of Philosophy and Scientific Method).

Wright, Georg Henrik von (1968) *An Essay in Deontic Logic and the General Theory of Action*, Amsterdam: North Holland (= Acta Philosophica Fennica, Fasc. 21).

Wright, Georg Henrik von (1971) *Explanation and Understanding*, Ithaca NY: Cornell University Press.